CULTURES OF THE WORLD®

AUSTRALIA

Vijeya & Sundran Rajendra

BENCHMARK BOOKS

MARSHALL CAVENDISH
NEW YORK

PICTURE CREDITS

Cover photo: © Robert Garvey/CORBIS

ANA Press Agency: 66, 73 • Peter Andrews: 35 • Australian Foreign Affairs: 129 • Australian High Commission, Singapore: 21, 23, 41, 54, 102, 116 • Australian Meat and Livestock: 121, 122, 125, 127 • Benaji Pty Ltd: 4, 7, 10, 13, 14, 16, 17, 27, 28, 31, 40, 53, 57, 58, 59, 61, 64, 70, 71, 72, 76, 94, 97, 100, 103, 106, 108, 109, 111, 112, 114, 115, 118, 124 • Oliver Bolch: 18 • Jan Butchofsky-Houser/Houserstock: 65 • Camera Press: 96 • Corbis: title • Haga Library, Japan: 84 • HBL Network: 86 • Dave G. Houser/Houserstock: 44 • Imagebank: 89 • International Photobank: 36, 52 • Ludo Kuipers/OzOutback Internet Services: 119 • Richard L'Anson: 67, 107 • Life File Photo Library: 4, 15, 22, 24, 25, 33, 38, 39, 68, 69, 82, 110, 113, 120 • Lonely Planet: 45, 117 • Loo Chuan Ming: 60 • Newspix: 29, 30, 93 • Orios Oven: 131 • Photobank: 6, 42, 88, 92 • Edward Stokes: 3, 8, 9, 11, 12, 19, 20, 34, 37, 43, 55, 56, 63, 74, 77, 79, 80, 83, 87, 90, 91, 98, 99, 104, 105 • Trip Photographic Library: 5, 46, 47, 48, 49, 50, 51, 78

ACKNOWLEDGMENTS

With thanks to Dr. Patricia O'Brien, Center for Australian and New Zealand Studies, Washington DC, and Ms. Kate Gorringe-Smith of Melbourne, Australia, for their expert reading of this manuscript. The authors would like to thank Rudi Rajendra for his assistance in preparing this book.

PRECEDING PAGE

Two young Australian girls, wearing T-shirts displaying the Australian Aboriginal Flag, show off their heritage.

Marshall Cavendish
99 White Plains Road
Tarrytown, NY 10591
Website: www.marshallcavendish.com

© Times Media Private Limited 1990, 2002
© Marshall Cavendish International (Asia) Private Limited 2004
All rights reserved. First edition 1990. Second edition 2002.

® "Cultures of the World" is a registered trademark of Marshall Cavendish Corporation.

Originated and designed by
Times Books International, an imprint of
Marshall Cavendish International (Asia) Private Limited,
a member of the Times Publishing Group

Library of Congress Cataloging-in-Publication Data
Rajendra, Vijeya, 1936–
    Australia / Vijeya Rajendra and Sundran Rajendra.—2nd ed.
        p. cm.—(Cultures of the world)
    Summary: Presents the history, geography, government, economy, environment, religion,
        people, and social life and customs of the island continent of Australia.
    Includes bibliographical references and index.
    ISBN 0-7614-1473-8
    1. Australia—Juvenile literature. [1. Australia.] I. Rajendra, Sundran, 1967-II. Title. III.
        Series
DU96.R34 2002
994—dc21   2002019206

7 6 5 4

CONTENTS

Australia has been called the "oldest continent" because much of its rock was formed 3.5 billion years ago in the Precambrian Age.

Australians are friendly and informal, and they are very fond of their animal emblem, the kangaroo.

Bush roads are dotted with signs showing Australia's unique animals.

INTRODUCTION

AUSTRALIA IS THE LAND "down under." Beyond kangaroos and koalas lies a vast continent of mystery and contradiction. From tropical rain forests to endless deserts, from golden beaches to ancient mountains, Australia is a land of flood and drought, heat and cold, fire and water.

The 19.4 million inhabitants of the continent of Australia live in one of the most cosmopolitan, highly urbanized states in the world. Today this young nation, built on the heritage of the West, is preparing to play a greater political role among its neighbors in Asia.

As a land of amazing and unique natural beauty, Australia is taking strict measures to conserve its fragile environment for future generations. Rich in natural resources, Australia continues to attract great numbers of immigrants from all over the world. The Aboriginal peoples are becoming more active in Australian society while preserving their traditional values, contributing their ancient heritage to Australia's young and multicultural society.

GEOGRAPHY

AUSTRALIA, the sixth largest country in the world, lies in the Southern Hemisphere, between 11° and 44° south latitude and 113° and 154° east longitude. Its population of 19.4 million inhabits an area of land about the same size as the continental United States. Mainland Australia, with an area of 2,967,909 square miles (7,686,884 square km), is so enormous that it is regarded as the world's seventh and smallest continent.

Australia has six states: Queensland, New South Wales, Victoria, Tasmania, South Australia, and Western Australia. It also has three internal territories—Northern Territory, Australian Capital Territory, and Jervis Bay Territory—and seven external territories—Christmas Island, Cocos Islands, Norfolk Island, Coral Sea Islands, Ashmore and Cartier Islands, Heard and McDonald Islands, and Australian Antarctic Territory.

Left: **In contrast to the central deserts, the coast offers a picture of lush vegetation.**

Opposite: **Everything in Australia is on a large scale. The spectacular Blue Mountains, near Sydney, offer a breathtaking view of Australia's beautiful natural landscape. The rock formation known as the Three Sisters is a famous feature of this mountain range.**

The Great Sandy Desert
in the northwest of the
country stretches as far
as the eye can see.

A LAND AS OLD AS TIME

The continent of Australia is often described as an "old land" because the geological activity that created the country's mountains, rivers, and plains ceased millions of years ago. Earthquakes are rare in Australia; the last volcanic eruption occurred more than 5,000 years ago. Over the centuries, wind and water have eroded the land's more spectacular features, leaving vast stretches of flat, featureless plains. The highest mountain in Australia, Mount Kosciusko, is only 7,310 feet (2,228 m) above sea level.

Mount Kosciusko lies in the southern part of the Eastern Highlands, a belt of elevated land stretching down the length of Australia's eastern coast from northern Queensland to central Victoria—a distance of 1,860 miles (2,992 km). Settlers first arriving in Australia called these highlands the Great Dividing Range since they were an obstacle blocking their exploration of the lands farther to the west.

Beyond the Great Dividing Range lie the great plains of the Central Lowlands. This area is remarkable for what lies underneath it—vast underground stores of water trapped in porous sandstone between beds of hard rock. Farmers use windmills to pump this water (called artesian water) to the surface to irrigate crops and water livestock.

The western two-thirds of the Australian continent is an arid, flat surface called the Great Western Plateau. This ancient region, rich in minerals such as iron ore, bauxite, and uranium, includes many deserts. One such desert is the 434-mile-wide (698-km-wide) Nullarbor Plain. Although it sounds like an Aboriginal name, Nullarbor is actually a Latin phrase (*nulla arbor*) meaning "no tree," in reference to its treeless landscape. Travelers can cross the plain on the Trans-Australian railroad, which has the longest stretch of straight railroad track in the world—297 miles (477 km).

Windmills pump artesian water to ground level. The water is then stored in reservoirs and used for irrigation and watering livestock.

THE GREAT BARRIER REEF

The Great Barrier Reef is an 82,800 square mile (214,452 square km) complex of islands and coral reefs stretching over 1,196 miles (1,924 km) along Australia's northeastern coast. Built by countless tiny coral polyps over 2 million years, it is the largest known coral formation in the world.

Today, the reef is one of the world's greatest tourist attractions. Visitors look at the coral through glass-bottom boats, and swimmers and divers (*below*) get a firsthand view of the amazing variety of creatures that inhabit the reef. There are clams so big their shells can be used as bath tubs. Colorful fish rest among the deadly tentacles of anemones. At night, ghost crabs scuttle across the reef's beaches in search of insects and small animals.

The Great Barrier Reef has been declared a national park to protect the coral and wildlife from human exploitation. Still, thousands of square miles of reef have been destroyed in recent years. The culprit is the crown-of-thorns starfish, which feeds on the polyps that form the reef, leaving behind large areas of dead, colorless coral that are soon swept away by the sea. In spite of attempts to destroy them, the starfish population has increased dramatically over the past few years.

CLIMATE

Because it spans both the tropical and temperate regions of the Southern Hemisphere, Australia experiences a variety of climates. The continent's desert interior gives way to tropical regions in the north. Bordering the desert is a dry region of semidesert that acts as a transition zone to the more humid regions of the north, east, and south. The southeastern coast, where most of Australia's population lives, is cooler and drier. The southwest is very hot and dry in the summer, but milder and wetter in the winter. The climate is similar to that of the Mediterranean countries of Europe, or of California in the United States.

Summers in Australia range from hot to very hot. Dry winds blowing from the west send temperatures in the country's interior soaring to over 104°F (40°C) during the summer months, which last from December to February in the Southern Hemisphere. Coastal regions are cooled by offshore breezes. Because of the heat and lack of rain, bushfires often rage through the landscape, destroying an average of 780 square miles (2,020 square km) of forest every year.

In the south of the country, temperatures drop considerably in the winter and frosts are common. During the winter months of June, July, and August, snow falls in the Eastern Highlands of Victoria and New South Wales. These highlands boast a number of ski resorts.

Bushfires, fanned by dry winds, burn up vast areas of forest and grassland.

More than 1,000 different types of plants grow on the Arnhem Land Plateau, located on the tip of the Northern Territory.

RAINFALL The high temperatures and low rainfall of the inland areas mean that 70 percent of Australia receives less than 20 inches (50 cm) of rain a year, making it the world's driest continent. Farming in these areas is difficult, but not impossible, thanks to the exploitation of artesian water and the construction of many irrigation projects. In contrast, the east, the southwesternern tip, and the tropical regions in the north are wetter. Cairns, a town on the northern coast of Queensland, receives more than 100 inches (250 cm) of rain a year. Located on the northeastern coast, Tully has Australia's highest annual rainfall—173 inches (440 cm).

In most areas of Australia, there are wide changes in rainfall from year to year. Droughts are common in the inland areas and may last for several years. Droughts affect all Australians as farming is a major source of wealth.

NATIVE ANIMALS

When the first Europeans arrived in Australia and started to explore the country, they could hardly believe the strange animals they saw. They, and the settlers who came after them, were especially fascinated by the various types of marsupials that they saw in Australia. Marsupials are mammals that raise their offspring in a pouch on their body until the youngsters are a reasonable size and can fend for themselves. These creatures have adapted to the harsh Australian environment. The marsupial family includes possums, koalas, kangaroos, wombats, and carnivores such as the fierce Tasmanian Devil.

Kangaroos are a common sight in the Australian countryside, or bush. Like other marsupials, female kangaroos carry their babies, called joeys, in a pouch located on their abdomen. Kangaroos move by hopping on their powerful hind legs. They can travel as far as 30 feet (9 m) in a single jump. When fighting, kangaroos lash out with their hind legs or punch with their smaller front paws. One kangaroo that escaped from a zoo in Adelaide knocked out a policeman with one punch before it was recaptured!

Above: **The kangaroo is the country's animal emblem.**

Below: **Tasmanian Devil has acquired a fierce reputation.**

UNIQUE CREATURES Unlike the kangaroo, which feeds on grass, the koala, another marsupial, only eats the leaves of the eucalyptus. Koalas spend most of their lives clinging to tree branches. When they are old enough to leave the pouch, koalas catch a ride on their mother's back. Koalas appear to be shy, cuddly creatures, but they have sharp claws. In Queensland, laws have been passed prohibiting visitors from holding the koala.

The most unusual creature of the bush is the duck-billed platypus. The platypus is one of two animals, the other being the echidra, in a group of animals unique to Australia—the monotremes. These are mammals that lay eggs. The platypus's body is covered with fur like that of other mammals, but it has a bill and webbed feet like a duck's.

Another remarkable animal is the mallee fowl, which builds its nest out of a mound of dirt. The female covers its eggs with dirt and keeps them at a constant temperature by adding or removing dirt.

OLD TOM

Inside the museum in Eden, a fishing town in New South Wales, is the skeleton of Old Tom, a killer whale, or orca, that formed an extraordinary partnership with local fishermen in the 19th century. These fishermen hunted whalebone whales, which migrated along Australia's eastern coast during winter.

Whenever a whale strayed close to Eden, Old Tom and his pack herded it into the town's bay. If no fishermen were around, some of the pack went to the shore and raised a terrific noise. The fishermen quickly recognized the signal to rush to their boats. While they were hurrying out, the orcas attacked the unfortunate whale. By the time the fishermen arrived, the whale was battered and exhausted and was easily killed. In return for their help, the fishermen allowed the killer pack to drag the dead whale to the sea bottom where they feasted on the tongue and lips. A day later the fishermen returned to tow the rest of the body to shore.

This bizarre partnership lasted nearly 90 years. But, after World War I, the orcas started to disappear. They were killed at sea by Norwegian sailors fishing off the coast. Once the killer whales were gone, the whalebone whales stopped coming into Eden. The town's whaling industry closed down. In 1930, Old Tom, by then well over 90 years old, made his last visit to Eden. The next day he was found dead, drifting in the bay. Local fishermen, who recognized their old friend, dragged his body to shore. The skeleton was sent to the town's museum where it remains on display to this day.

The emu is a flightless bird, the second largest in the world after the ostrich.

The largest bird in Australia is the emu. Its typical diet consists of seeds, fruits, insects, and the new shoots of plants. The emu is unusual in that the male incubates the eggs.

Australia has several highly dangerous native animals. The venom of the tiger snake of southern Australia is so deadly that one drop can kill a person. The bite of the tiny red-back spider is also highly toxic. It makes its home in sheltered nooks and crannies, and has even been discovered under the toilet seat in bathrooms in the bush! Since European settlement, there have been over 150 recorded fatalities from shark attacks alone.

Above: **The duck-billed platypus seems to have the characteristics of both mammals and birds.**

Opposite: **Contrary to popular belief, the koala is not a bear, but a marsupial. The koala feeds exclusively on the leaves of the eucalyptus.**

15

The boab is quite common in northern Australia, where it is also called the bottle tree.

NATIVE VEGETATION

Australia's coastal regions boast the most luxuriant vegetation. A major physical feature of the continent is the chain of mountain ranges which runs just inland from the southern and eastern coast. From the height of these ranges to the coast lie Australia's heaviest forests. A second great forest belt also stretches 350 miles (563 km) through southwestern Western Australia.

In the north, these forests are typically monsoon forests, similar to the forests of Indonesia and Malaysia. Queensland and the northeastern parts

of Cape York Peninsula exhibit the most exotic vegetation. In the cooler south, there are coastal and mallee woodlands and cool temperature rainforests. Forests found in the corner of southwestern Australia are rich in vegetation, and many of the plants found here are unique to Australia. The forests in Tasmania resemble those found in New Zealand and South America. Inland, as the climate becomes more arid, the forests are replaced by shrublands, savannah woodlands, and grasslands.

Australia's national flowers is the golden wattle, which belongs to the Acacia family. In spring, the golden wattle produces large clusters of tiny golden flowers. Another striking plant is the flame tree of the coastal rainforests on the Eastern Highlands. From a distance, its bright red flowers create the illusion that the tree is on fire.

It is from the golden wattle that Australia draws its national colors: gold and green. It is the first flower of spring, and the wattle thrives despite bushfires and harsh conditions.

HISTORY

AUSTRALIA'S INDIGENOUS PEOPLE probably migrated to Australia from Southeast Asia 40,000 years ago. At that time, Australia was still joined to the continent of Asia by a string of small islands.

Sailing south in canoes, the migrants landed on the northern coast of Australia and then moved southward across the rest of the new land. Europeans who came to Australia later called the original settlers "aborigines," meaning indigenous inhabitants.

By the time the first British colonists arrived in Australia in 1788, the population of Aborigines had grown to about 300,000. Nevertheless, the British colonists declared the land *terra nullius*, meaning land uninhabited by humans!

Left: **The oldest known remains of Aboriginal people, dating back at least 35,000 years, were discovered at Lake Mungo in New South Wales, the site of an ancient lake that has since dried up.**

Opposite: **When the British first colonized Australia, they used it as a penal settlement. Criminals were sent by the hundreds to serve their prison sentence in Australia.**

Above: **The Aborigines made rock paintings to pass their stories from one generation to the next.**

Below: **The boomerang.**

NOMADS

The Aborigines were nomads living in family clans, each with its own territory where it could camp, hunt, and fish. They burned large tracts of forest to provide grazing land for giant kangaroos and other animals that are now extinct; these were killed and eaten. The Aboriginal hunters brought two useful aids from their original homeland—the dingo, a hunting dog that could not bark—and the boomerang—a v-shaped wooden wing that could be thrown over great distances. When hurled into the wind, the boomerang's aerodynamic shape made it travel on an arc-shaped path and eventually return to the thrower. The boomerang was used to hunt animals.

Aborigines were very effective hunters. The secret of their success lay in their wise use of natural resources. They occupied land in a productive way, moving on with climatic changes and in response to environmental demands. Today, their methods of finding food and water are taught to soldiers, to help them survive in Australia's inhospitable interior. Although they did not build permanent settlements or carry many possessions, the Aborigines recorded their history and culture in paintings on rocks and caves using charcoal, clay, and ocher. Archaeologists have also found evidence of regular contact between Aboriginal hunters and Indonesian traders from the north.

TERRA AUSTRALIS INCOGNITA

For many thousands of years, the Aborigines were the only people to visit Australia. Europeans, however, suspected that a "great southern land" existed. Such a land, they reasoned, was needed to balance the weight of the land in the Northern Hemisphere and prevent the world from tipping over! This land was called *Terra Australis Incognita*, a Greek phrase meaning the "unknown southern land." This phrase was first used by the Egyptian geographer Ptolemy who, in the second century, sketched a map of the known coasts of Asia and a big unknown piece of land to the south.

British officers toast the hoisting of the Union Jack on Australian soil, claiming the land for England.

Seventeenth-century Dutch merchants sailing the trade routes to the East Indies were the first Europeans to set foot in Australia. When the British learned of their reports, they were keen to claim the land for themselves.

In 1768 they sent a man on a secret mission. The man's name was James Cook. Publicly, he was preparing to visit Tahiti to observe the planet Venus. But Cook had secret orders to find the southern land and claim it for England. He first sighted Australia in April 1770. He spent about four months mapping the eastern coast, describing the flora and fauna, and attempting to make contact with the natives, the Aborigines.

A log cabin from the 1830s. The early settlers had to clear large areas of bush to build their cabins.

SETTLING IN

Although news of Cook's voyage caused a sensation in London, more than 10 years passed before the government decided to establish a colony in Australia. It was to be a penal colony. At that time Britain had a serious crime problem. The government decided to reduce overcrowding in British jails by sending convicts to Australia. This system was known as transportation.

The first colony was set up in Sydney Cove in 1788. In the beginning, life was very hard for the new settlers. Their crops did not do well. Their cattle were stolen by the Aborigines, and food had to be rationed.

Nevertheless, conditions gradually improved and the colony grew. Other settlements were built along the coast of New South Wales and in Tasmania. Between 1788 and 1868, 160,000 convicts were sent to Australia. With them came thousands of free settlers, people who chose to escape poverty and unemployment in Europe and take their chances in Australia. The new migrants increased the status of the colony and encouraged the growth of industry and farming.

By 1859 five colonies had grown along the coast of Australia: New South Wales, Tasmania, Queensland, Victoria, and South Australia. Each colony had its own governor, laws, trade policies, police, and transportation system. Relations among the colonies were not good. A fierce rivalry existed among the older colonies, and very few people ever visited other colonies.

Australia's vast inland had scarcely been mapped. A number of explorers, some sent by the colonial authorities, set about finding out what lay within the country's enormous interior. The men chosen for these expeditions had to be brave and persevering. They had to travel for months in desolate, unknown country, had to repel attacks from hostile Aborigines, and had somehow to find their way back home. Understandably, many of these men never returned.

The discovery of gold in 1851 caused a frantic gold rush. One year later, 95,000 new settlers flooded into New South Wales and Victoria.

Elizabeth Beckford, 70, was sentenced to seven years' transportation for stealing 11 pounds (5 kg) of cheese. James Freeman was condemned to death for robbery when he was 16 years old; the sentence was later changed to seven years' transportation. James Grace was just 11 years old when he was sentenced to seven years' transportation; he had been caught stealing a pair of silk stockings.

CRIME AND PUNISHMENT

Stealing a buckle or a loaf of bread was enough for a person to be sentenced to a life of exile in a penal settlement such as Port Arthur (*above*) in Tasmania. Thus Australia became a dumping ground of petty thieves, Irish rebels, and prostitutes.

THE SQUATTERS

Settlers took advantage of the new lands opened up by explorers. They brought flocks of sheep and drove them inland to graze on the newly discovered grasslands. Since these farmers did not buy the land they used, but instead declared their claim to the government, they were called squatters. Squatting was far from easy. Besides the constant threats of drought, bushfires, and floods, squatters had to deal with attacks from Aborigines and armed robbers called bushrangers. Their success depended on how many workers they could hire and also on the fluctuating price of wool in London. Worse than all this was the isolation. Loneliness and boredom sent many men back to the towns to find a bride. The wives of squatters faced a tough life. They had to endure poverty, isolation, and danger. Supplies and mail, often brought by ox wagons, came a few times a year, weather allowing. Women who could not shoot a gun or ride a horse were scorned and were at a real disadvantage when it came to fending off attacks by Aborigines.

The hard work and sacrifice of the squatters paid off when their wool fetched high prices on the London market. The local "squattocracy" owned comfortable homes and vast areas of land.

Forceful measures were taken by white settlers in their quest for development. Tribes, clans, and families were dispersed by the land grab.

CLASHES WITH THE ABORIGINES Fighting between Aborigines and white settlers became increasingly common. The squatters had taken over the Aborigines' traditional hunting lands. Their nomadic way of life was disrupted and would never again be the same. Since they were unable to get their food the traditional way, the Aborigines fought back by stealing the squatters' sheep. They also attacked the squatters' homes and families. The squatters in turn killed whole tribes of Aboriginal men, women, and children. A century after the First Fleet (the fleet of ships that transported the first British settlers to Australia) arrived in Australia, the Aboriginal population had been reduced from 300,000 to 80,000.

THE LEGEND OF NED KELLY

"Edward Kelly, I hereby sentence you to death by hanging. May the Lord have mercy on your soul!" When Ned Kelly, Australia's most famous outlaw and leader of the Kelly Gang, heard these words, he replied to the judge, "Yes, I will meet you there!" Strangely enough, the judge died two weeks later.

In 1878 Kelly allegedly shot a policeman after stealing a horse. In the next two years, he and his gang hid out in the Wombat Ranges in Victoria, in between two daring raids on local banks. Kelly soon became a folk hero, regarded by many as a man fighting against an unfair system that was indifferent to Australia's poor and underprivileged classes.

Kelly's boldest move also proved to be his undoing. He and his gang tried to destroy the police train passing through Glenrowan. One of his captives managed to escape and inform the police, who soon surrounded the town. For hours, nothing stirred. Then, out of the darkness strode a giant figure clad in metal, with guns blazing. The policemen's bullets seemed to bounce off the creature, but the giant eventually collapsed. When the policemen removed the armor, they realized it was Kelly. After killing the members of the gang, the troopers took Kelly, who was still alive, to Melbourne, where he was sentenced and hanged on November 11, 1880. He was 25 years old.

BUDDING NATION

On the first day of the 20th century, the states put aside their differences and joined to form the Commonwealth of Australia. Federation and nationhood for the six colonies were not a revolt against the old order, but rather a coming-of-age.

However, like many other countries in the first half of the 20th century, the new nation soon found itself face to face with the double burden of war and depression.

Australia, as a member of the British Empire, automatically followed Great Britain's declaration of war on Germany in 1914. In the next four years, more than 330,000 Australian men volunteered for service in Europe, the Middle East, New Guinea, and the Indian Ocean. On April 25, 1915, Australian soldiers took part in their most famous battle: the Gallipoli campaign. Masterminded by Winston Churchill and involving an army of Australian and New Zealand soldiers (called Anzacs), it proved to be a disaster from the very beginning. Australians, however, commemorate the battle every year on Anzac Day, the day when Australians first fought for their new nation. A source of pride to their countrymen, Australians remember the Anzacs as "the finest body of men brought together in modern times."

Anzac Day commemorates the battle in 1915, when the heroic Anzac troops were defeated by the Turks and Germans.

Nicknamed "The Coathanger," the Sydney Harbor Bridge is the largest span bridge in the world. Its main span measures 1,660 feet (506 m) and contains 52,000 tons of steel. For the bicentenary celebrations, Sydney Harbor was filled with sailing ships of all shapes and sizes, including a reconstruction of the First Fleet.

LAND OF OPPORTUNITY

After World War I, Australia opened its doors to emigrants from Britain and Europe. For the next 50 years, immigrants came to Australia in large numbers. New labor and new markets made the country rich in the 1920s. This period of prosperity ended in 1929 when Australia, along with the United States and many other countries, was affected by the worldwide economic depression. One of the few bright spots during those years was the opening of Sydney's famous Harbor Bridge in 1932. Work on the bridge had started nearly a decade earlier. Over the years, Sydney's inhabitants looked on in wonder as the huge single arch was slowly completed. Despite the hard times, more than 350,000 people flocked to Sydney to catch a glimpse of the bridge when it was declared open.

World War II, which began in 1939, resulted in closer relations between the United States and Australia. After losing the Philippines to Japanese forces, the United States set up its Pacific base in Australia. One million troops were stationed in Melbourne and Brisbane between 1942–45. Many Australians believe it was the U.S. army presence that prevented

Australia from being invaded by the Japanese. Twenty years after World War II, Australian and American soldiers fought together in Vietnam. Soldiers returning from this controversial war were often booed by crowds. Today, Vietnam War veterans are recognized and honored.

In recent years Australia's attitude toward communist countries has relaxed. In fact, Australia was the first Western nation to officially recognize the People's Republic of China. Many Australian goods are sold to China and the former Soviet Union. Presently, Australia is trying to create closer cultural and economic ties with its neighbors, particularly Southeast Asia and the Pacific Islands. The government spends millions of dollars on foreign aid to countries like the Philippines and Indonesia. Nevertheless, Australia still maintains a strong relationship with the United States as well as its traditional ties with Britain.

In 1988 Australia celebrated its bicentenary—the 200th anniversary of the arrival of the First Fleet. The World Expo was held in Brisbane that year. In 2000, Sydney hosted the Olympic Games. Australians are aware of how much they have accomplished in the past and how much still lies ahead.

The opening ceremony for the 2000 Olympic Games in Sydney.

GOVERNMENT

AUSTRALIA IS A FEDERATION of states with a parliamentary system of government. Australia can be called a constitutional monarchy as it recognizes the queen of England as the head of state. The British monarchy is represented in Australia by a governor-general and six state governors.

FEDERAL GOVERNMENT

Power rests with the elected political party that holds the majority in the House of Representatives. The leader is the prime minister. Government is modeled on the British system of two governing bodies: a legislative assembly (the House of Representatives) and a council of review (the Senate). The Senate consists of 76 members who are elected every six years. The House of Representatives has 150 members and they face elections every three years.

Although Australia's constitution gives the House of Representatives the right to enact laws, they must be passed by a majority in the Senate before they become law. Additionally, any laws that involve changes to the constitution must be decided by a referendum in which the country's citizens vote on whether or not they want such changes to take place. History has shown that Australians are not eager to alter the constitution that has served them so well—of the 42 proposals put to a vote in 18 referenda, only eight have been passed.

Above: **Australia's Parliament House in Canberra.**

Opposite: **The House of Representatives in session.**

SYMBOLS OF A NATION

The national flag (*above left*) consists of a small Union Jack, representing Australia's historical link with Britain; the five stars of the Southern Cross constellation (a prominent feature of the night sky in the Southern Hemisphere); and the seven-pointed star, which represents Australia's six states and its group of territories. The Red Ensign, a red version of the national flag, is used by merchant ships registered in Australia. The national coat of arms (*above right*) consists of a shield divided into six sections, each containing a state badge, surrounded by an ermine border, signifying the federation of the states into one nation. The shield is supported by two native animals, an emu on the right and a kangaroo, Australia's national animal emblem, on the left. These two animals were chosen for the coat of arms because neither can move backwards, thus symbolizing the eternal progress of the nation. They are resting on a branch of golden wattle, Australia's floral emblem.

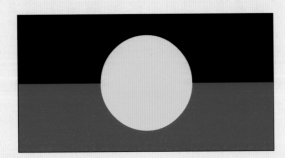

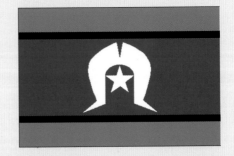

On July 14, 1995, the Australian Aboriginal flag (*above left*) and the Torres Strait Islander flag (*above right*) were proclaimed as additional official flags of Australia under the Flags Act.

THE REGIONAL LEVEL

Each of Australia's states is administered by a parliament, which consists of a legislative council (similar to the federal Senate) and a legislative assembly (similar to the House of Representatives). The premier is the leader of the political party dominating the legislative assembly. State parliaments existed long before the creation of the federal government in 1901 and, therefore, retain many of their former powers. In addition to collecting state taxes and duties, each state runs schools and hospitals, administers its own laws, and has its own police force.

Cities and shires (counties) are governed by local councils headed by mayors. The local council's responsibilities include town planning, waste management, and road construction.

The Western Australian coat of arms outside the law courts of Perth. The swan on the shield is Perth's animal emblem.

Australians enjoy full democratic rights, including free speech. These protestors are occupying the site of a future uranium mine in South Australia.

PARTICIPATING IN A DEMOCRACY

Australia has a short but strong tradition of democracy. Since members of all levels of government are elected by the people, most citizens find themselves visiting a voting booth at least once a year. Unlike in other democracies, including the United States, Britain, and France, voting in Australia is compulsory for all adults 18 years old and above. Citizens who are overseas or otherwise unable to vote in person at a polling center are required to mail in an absentee vote. Those who do not vote are fined.

All elections held in Australia use a procedure known as the preferential voting system, in which voters assign an order to each candidate. The candidate of their choice would be first, followed by their second choice, and so on. Because of this detailed procedure, it takes several days to count all the votes. After an election, members of the ruling party elect a prime minister or, in the case of a state, a premier, who then appoints a cabinet of ministers, each responsible for a particular area of government, such as defense, education, or welfare.

POLITICAL PARTIES

There are four major political parties in Australia.

THE AUSTRALIAN LABOR PARTY The nation's oldest party, it was started in 1891 by sheep shearers unhappy with their pay and working conditions. The party of the working people, it has a strong tradition of democratic socialism, pioneering such reforms as pensions and minimum wages.

THE LIBERAL PARTY OF AUSTRALIA After its founding in 1944, the party dominated federal politics for two decades. Liberals believe in free enterprise and the freedom to conduct their lives with minimum government interference. To this end, they support the reduction of taxes and restrictions on trade and business. On March 2, 1996, the Liberal–National Party coalition won the federal election, ending 13 years of Labor Party government. John Howard (*right*) then became the prime minister. In November 2001, he again won the elections to remain prime minister, taking him to a third term in office.

THE NATIONAL PARTY OF AUSTRALIA Known as the National Country Party at the time of its creation in 1919, it is the champion of primary industries such as farming and mining. The party draws its membership primarily from Australia's rural population. Since 1949, the National Party and Liberal Party have combined forces in both state and federal parliaments to form ruling coalitions.

THE AUSTRALIAN DEMOCRATS Formed in 1977 by Don Chipp, the party was set up to keep a check on the other major parties, or in the more colorful words of Senator Chipp, "to keep the bastards honest."

THE REPUBLICAN DEBATE

Australians' desire for a republic seems to be growing, especially among the young. The Australian Republican Movement (ARM) argues that changes to the constitution and the Australian system of democracy should be minimal. Severing ties with the Commonwealth is also not favored by ARM.

Opinion polls have shown that while the majority of Australians are in favor of a republic (as opposed to constitutional monarchy), they are not in favor of adopting the U.S. or French systems. However, the final step toward complete self-government failed when Australians rejected the November 1999 referendum to make Australia a republic with an Australian head of state. The queen of England continues to be Australia's head of state.

ECONOMY

AUSTRALIANS HAVE traditionally relied on exports to maintain one of the highest standards of living in the world. Australia is the world's leading supplier of several important commodities such as aluminum, wool, beef and veal, coal, mineral sands, live goats and sheep, and refined lead. An old saying went that Australia's economic fortunes "ride on the sheep's back," in reference to the fact that the nation has relied on the export of primary resources, such as sheep, cattle, and minerals, to create wealth. Although Australian wool is famous throughout the world, the country's wool production fell by 35 percent in the 1990s.

Opposite and above: **Livestock is raised in the vast areas of dry inland country, where the animals are left to run wild on the land.**

Global economic trends indicate that Australia's dependence on the export of raw materials may threaten its future prosperity. For the past few years the country has been trying to diversify the economy by reducing its dependence on the export of agricultural and mining products.

Australia is trying to develop other exports that can effectively compete in international markets. To encourage overseas trade and investment, in the 1980s the government restructured the national economy to force domestic industry to become more competitive. The focus of trade was shifted to the rapidly growing markets in Southeast Asia. Attention was also paid to schools and universities to ensure that future graduates were equipped with the necessary skills to aid industry. Long known as the "lucky country" because of its natural wealth, Australia is aiming to become, through the hard work and ingenious efforts of its people, the "clever country."

The World Trade Center in Melbourne. Australia is a major player in international trade.

TRADING PARTNERS

Australia trades with both developed and developing nations. Japan is its biggest customer, buying more than a quarter of all Australian exports. Australia's major exports to Japan are minerals, fuels, and agricultural products. Another close trading partner is Southeast Asia, which accounts for more than a third of Australia's exports. Japan and the United States are Australia's largest suppliers, usually of capital equipment. Products from these two countries make up nearly half of all Australian imports.

MINERALS AND ENERGY

Australia is a land of incredible mineral wealth. Its deposits of coal, which can satisfy the demands of the whole world for several centuries, is the nation's single largest export earner. Australia is the largest producer of aluminum, most of which is mined along the western coast of the Cape York Peninsula, and the second largest exporter of iron ore. Copper, lead, zinc, gold, and silver are also mined in substantial quantities, along with natural gas, uranium, titanium, and precious gems. The income earned from minerals, metals, and fuels accounts for 50 percent of export earnings and includes the annual export of 81.5 million tons of coal, 88 million tons of iron ore, and 9 million tons of aluminum ore to Japan, Southeast Asia, China, and the European Union. Still, it is estimated that only 0.01 percent of the continent's vast reserves has so far been mined.

Australia is one of the world's biggest producers of minerals and metals. Beneath the dry barren soil lies a wealth of minerals and energy resources.

BURIED TREASURE

Ninety-five percent of the opals (*below*) and half of the sapphires
that reach the world's markets come from Australia. The world's
largest opal mine is near Coober Pedy, a town in South Australia.
Because temperatures in the district often exceed 104°F (40°C),
many of the townspeople live in underground homes dug into the
dry earth. The Argyle mines in the Kimberley Ranges, Western
Australia, produce most of the world's diamonds.

Gold has been mined in great quantities in the states of
Victoria, Queensland, Western Australia, and New South Wales
since the gold rushes of the 1850s. A number of massive nuggets
have been found, including the
205-pound (93-kg) Holtermann
nugget and the 78-pound
(35-kg) Welcome Stranger.

In 1931, the body of
Harold Lasseter was found
in the Northern Territory.
Lasseter had earlier
claimed to have found
a fabulous mile-long
(1.6 km-long) reef
of gold. Although a
number of adventurers
have tried and failed
to find Lasseter's Reef,
it is widely believed
that the reef and its
incredible wealth
do exist, and are
waiting some-
where in the
Outback to
be found.

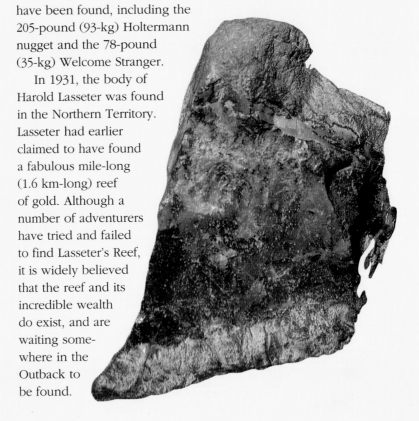

AGRICULTURE

Despite Australia's mostly arid soil and dry climate, agricultural exports, including wheat, wool, beef, sugar, and dairy products, earn approximately a third of Australia's national income. This success is in part due to limited domestic demand because of the nation's small population and the application of sophisticated farming techniques to semiarid lands. Sheep ranches, known as "stations," in Australia's inland stock 12 head of sheep for every square mile. Such stations are tens of thousands of acres in size. Most of Australia's 150 million sheep are raised for their wool.

Because of Australia's unpredictable climate and the continual fluctuation in international demand for agricultural products, the volume and value of Australia's agricultural produce vary greatly from year to year. The nation's farmers cope with the unpredictable market by rapidly changing to new crops and livestock as the need arises. In 1999 the agricultural sector was favored by strong domestic demand, low interest rates, and low inflation. In subsequent years, however, the economy slowed down, following the general trend of the global economy.

With the help of modern equipment, Australian farmers are able to harvest large quantities of grain. Wheat is one of the country's main crops.

Australia boasts one of the world's largest reserves of minerals.

MANUFACTURING

In addition to its steel works and aluminum smelters, Australia's major manufacturing industries include clothing and textiles, chemicals, aeronautical equipment, and electronics. The local motor vehicle industry produces 3 million cars a year. Four of the largest international vehicle makers—Ford, General Motors, Mitsubishi, and Toyota—have factories in Australia, producing more than 300,000 units a year.

TOURISM

In recent years, Australia has been riding the crest of an unprecedented wave of popularity among international travelers. More than 2 million tourists visit Australia annually, spending millions of dollars during their stay. Revenue from tourism amounts to $2.7 billion every year. It is the largest industry in Australia, providing directly or indirectly more than 441,000 jobs. Most visitors come from the United States and New Zealand, as well as Britain, Germany, and Japan.

Australia is one of the world's most attractive countries to visit. Most visitors make it a point to go to Ayers Rock, now referred to by its Aboriginal name, Uluru.

TOURISM'S BAKER'S DOZEN

Australia's 13 most popular tourist attractions for overseas visitors are:

1. Sydney Opera House and The Rocks, Sydney
2. Darling Harbor, Sydney
3. Sydney Harbor and beaches, Sydney
4. Sydney Tower, Sydney
5. Surfers Paradise, Gold Coast
6. Blue Mountains, New South Wales
7. Taronga Park Zoo, Sydney
8. Queen Victoria Markets, Melbourne
9. New South Wales Art Gallery and Museum, Sydney
10. Royal Botanical Gardens, Melbourne
11. Seaworld, Gold Coast
12. King's Park, Perth
13. Jupiter's Casino, Gold Coast

ENVIRONMENT

GREETED BY A VAST and old continent, Australia's early settlers must have felt that the land was inexhaustible and unalterable. But unfortunately, 200 years of uncontrolled hunting and land clearing as well as water and air pollution have caused the destruction of unique ecosystems and the extinction of many plants and animals, fundamentally changing the face of Australia's landscape. One of the biggest challenges for Australians in the new millennium will be to use their land in a sustainable way by reducing greenhouse gas emissions and exploring renewable energy sources.

Opposite: **The unique shape of this tree in the Menindee Wetlands of New South Wales is the result of seasonal flooding.**

Left: **Dugongs, or sea cows, are in danger of extinction. Dugongs have been hunted illegally, caught in fishermen's shark nets, and hit by boats.**

THE THREAT TO BIODIVERSITY

Biodiversity, or biological diversity, refers to the variety of plants and animals found in a specific area. Australia has an extraordinarily high number of species of plants and animals, and many of them are unique to the country. This biodiversity is, however, under threat. Already 19 of the original mammal species are extinct, among them the Tasmanian tiger and certain species of bandicoots, wallabies, and native mice. One fifth of the native mammals are currently threatened with extinction, including the blue whale, the southern right whale, dugongs, bettongs, potoroos, bats, and moles. Half of Australia's land-based birds are predicted to become extinct by the year 2100. Of the 15,638 original species of plants, 83 are known to be extinct.

A Queensland red-necked wallaby and her young.

There are several reasons why so many of Australia's native plants and animals are endangered.

Australia has cleared more forests than any other developed country in the world. Many native animals die during the process of clearing or, afterward, because their habitats are destroyed. Many native animals are forced to compete for food with increasing numbers of sheep and cattle, animals that have been introduced to Australia for their economic value in the world market.

A further threat to Australia's biodiversity is mining. The country's rich mineral reserves produce vast amounts of gold, silver, copper, nickel, and other minerals. Mineral exports earn billions of dollars for Australia, but mining often has devastating effects on the country's environment. Open-cut mining methods use massive machines to demolish whole mountains in order to get to the underlying minerals.

Australia's largest river is the Murray. It is 1,566 miles (2,520 km) long. When combined with the Darling, it forms the Murray-Darling Basin (*above*), which extends over 15 percent of the continent and supports about one third of Australia's agricultural production. The Murray-Darling Basin suffers serious salinity problems due to land clearing and poor irrigation practices.

Harmful gases pumped into the atmosphere contribute to the greenhouse effect, which causes changes in the earth's climate.

THE OZONE HOLE

Greenhouse gases such as carbon dioxide, methane, and nitrous oxide get trapped in the atmosphere and contribute to global warming. Changing weather patterns and rising sea levels have also been linked to global warming.

In spite of its small population, Australia is a large producer of greenhouse gases. The country is responsible for about 2 percent of the world's total emissions. Most greenhouse gases produced by Australia come from the burning of fossil fuels such as coal, petroleum, and natural gas. Land clearing, which removes trees that absorb carbon dioxide, has also contributed to higher levels of greenhouse gases. However, Australia, along with the United States, decided in 2001 not to sign the the Kyoto Protocol to reduce greenhouse gases. Environmental activists have severely criticized Prime Minister John Howard on this issue.

Excessive production of another group of airborne pollutants—chloroflourocarbons, or CFCs—on a global scale has depleted ozone in the atmosphere, resulting in a hole in the ozone layer. This hole allows ultraviolet radiation to penetrate the earth's atmosphere, causing serious health problems, such as an increased risk of skin cancer. Australia already has the highest rate of skin cancer in the world. In recent years, the government has made efforts to educate the public about the dangers of overexposure to the sun and the benefits of wearing hats and sunscreen lotions.

PROTECTING THE ENVIRONMENT

As the effects of land clearing and pollution have become evident, more Australians are playing an active role in protecting and sustaining their environment.

Uranium mining is a source of intense controversy in Australia. Almost 15 percent of the world's uranium comes from Australia, and there is still potential for growth. In 1984 a Nuclear Disarmament Party was formed to lobby against the use of atomic weapons and the mining of uranium for making weapons of war.

Nevertheless, in 1996 Prime Minister John Howard's government abandoned a policy that restricted uranium production to only three sites in the country. The government recently announced that a new uranium mine at Jabiluka, in the heart of Australia's Kakadu National Park, is now under consideration.

Protection of old-growth forests, or forests that have been kept intact since early European settlement, is an important issue. Logging companies are eager to exploit the large trees as timber. The woodchipping industry, in which small pieces of wood are used to make paper and particle board, is another source of concern. Conservationists argue that woodchipping threatens wildlife habitats, causes soil erosion, and pollutes rivers.

The conservation movement in Australia remains strong. Many Australians support Greenpeace, the Wilderness Society, the Australian Conservation Foundation, and the Green Party.

An old-growth forest in Tasmania's Weldorough Reserve.

MANAGING WASTE

As is the case around the world, Australia's major cities are fighting the ongoing problem of waste disposal. Educating people to discard their trash in a responsible way has met with some success. Nevertheless, litter continues to clog rivers and streams.

Some of the garbage is not biodegradeable, which means it cannot be broken down by living organisms. Moreover, it attracts blowflies, rats, and other disease-carrying animals and insects. Landfills are unable to cope with the amount of garbage, and much industrial waste is hazardous.

Environmental groups have encouraged government councils to introduce organized ways to dispose of household waste. Local councils now provide recycling bins that are picked up by waste management authorities.

One day a year is set aside for a massive cleanup. On "Clean up Australia Day," people across the nation volunteer their time to remove litter from beaches, parks, and other public spaces. The first "Clean up Australia Day" was organized in 1989 in Sydney Harbor by Australian Ian Kiernan. The clean up day movement has since been taken up in over 120 countries.

ALTERNATIVE ENERGY SOURCES

Australians are experimenting with the use of alternative energy sources such as the sun, the wind, and rivers.

Sunny days are plentiful in Australia and solar power technology has enormous potential. Already, many Australian homes have solar-powered systems that heat water and generate electricity. These systems were a popular feature in the athletes' village at the 2000 Sydney Olympic Games, nicknamed the Green Games. Large-scale solar-based thermal power stations are being planned. Many telephone systems in remote areas of Australia are already powered by the sun. In 1999 scientists at the University of New South Wales were awarded a prize for developing the world's most efficient photovoltaic solar cell. These cells, which directly convert sunlight into electricity, are now commercially available worldwide.

About one sixth of Australia's electricity is produced by hydropower. Power is generated when water from a storage dam flows down through turbines. The Snowy Mountains Scheme, which was built in Australia with the help of immigrants in the 1950s and 1960s, is Australia's biggest hydroelectricity project. One drawback of such projects is that large tracts of land often need to be flooded to make an artificial dam. In the 1980s the damming of the Gordon River in Tasmania was stopped because of concerns by conservationists that native habitats would be destroyed.

Wind farms can be found in Australia, particularly in the windy coastal areas. The wind turbines are tall structures, often more than 98 feet (30 m) high, and can generate significant amounts of electricity.

Above: **Solar panels take advantage of Australia's plentiful sunlight to produce electricity at a tourist hotel near Uluru.**

Opposite: **A man dumps garbage in a landfill site.**

AUSTRALIANS

LURED BY THE OPPORTUNITY for wealth and freedom in the "lucky country," people from all parts of the world come to Australia to start a new life. It is estimated that about 100,000 immigrants come to Australia every year. In recent years, illegal immigrants from underdeveloped countries have tried to enter Australia by boat, often with the help of people smugglers.

Today, Australia's traditional British heritage is giving way to a multicultural society—a melting pot of peoples from more than 100 ethnic backgrounds, speaking 90 different languages, and practicing over 80 separate religions.

Left: **Australia is an immigrant society. For this family, citizenship day is the beginning of a new life in their adopted homeland. The certificate of citizenship is often kept as a precious document.**

Opposite: **After a steady decline, the Aboriginal population has started to increase in recent years.**

53

The Victorian Arts Center in Melbourne. State capitals attract most Australians because of the wide variety of activities they offer—from jobs to high-quality entertainment.

POPULATION DISTRIBUTION

Australia is one of the most highly urbanized countries in the world. Eighty-five percent of the country's population—about 16 million people—live in cities and large towns. They live mostly in Sydney, Melbourne, and Brisbane, the nation's three largest capital cities. Sydney, the capital of New South Wales, is Australia's largest city, with a population of 4 million. Melbourne is only slightly smaller, with 3.5 million inhabitants. The third largest is Brisbane, with more than 1.5 million residents. Australia's farmers, responsible for much of the nation's wealth, are only about 5 percent of the population.

About 40 percent of all Australians are under 25 years of age. But longer life expectancies and lower birth rates have meant that Australians on average are getting older. In 1996, 12 percent of the population was over 65 years old. By 2016, this age group is expected to grow to 16 percent. The growing number of older people in the country is expected to raise the demand for health services and public welfare in the near future as Australia's 9.2 million-strong workforce dwindles. Although Australia is a nation of active people, a diet high in meat has taken a toll on their health. Figures vary, but it is estimated that nearly one in two people is overweight, a contributing factor to heart disease and stroke.

Australia is a young nation with a young population. This is expected to change in the next few decades. Better healthcare and a lower birthrate will result in the older population out-numbering the younger groups.

The Chinese community celebrates Chinese New Year with lively lion dances in the streets of Sydney's Chinatown.

BUILDING A MULTICULTURAL SOCIETY

In the last century Australians saw themselves as 98 percent "British." The white population was overwhelmingly Anglo-Saxon and Celtic. The goldrushes of the 1850s doubled the nation's population within a few years and brought immigrants from a variety of ethnic backgrounds, including many Chinese. Although a large number returned to their homeland after the gold ran out, others chose to stay. Descendants of Chinese workers (known as ABCs, or Australian-Born Chinese) have lived in Australia for several generations and have large and well-organized communities. Chinese food has also become a part of Australian culture— nearly every town, large or small, boasts a Chinese restaurant.

The arrival of the early immigrants caused concern among much of the white population, leading to the enactment of the "White Australia"

immigration policy in 1901, designed to exclude non-European immigrants. This policy was abandoned in 1973. Migrants coming to the country at the end of World War II were therefore mainly European, particularly Italian, Greek, Yugoslavian, and German. The first Asian people to settle in Australia from the mid-1970s onward were Vietnamese "boat people"—refugees fleeing the communist regime in their homeland. Since then, many immigrants have come from Southeast Asia, India, the Philippines, Japan, China, and Hong Kong, bringing valuable skills to the nation.

In 1996 Federal Member of Parliament Pauline Hanson made a controversial speech on Asian immigration and Aboriginal affairs, which led to the formation of a right-wing political party called One Nation. Only a minority of Australians support One Nation, which did not perform well in the November 2001 federal election.

For a long time, the "White Australia" policy discriminated against nonwhite immigrants. However, recent Asian immigrants have added diversity to the country's social landscape, turning it into a multiethnic society.

OLD PEOPLE IN A NEW LAND

In 1988, while most of the Australian population was celebrating the 200th anniversary of European settlement in Australia, a section of the community declared a year of mourning. They were Australia's early inhabitants, the Aborigines. Like the indigenous peoples of many other countries, the Aborigines were persecuted by European settlers who, when they failed to annihilate the Aboriginal population, tried instead to annihilate their culture and to force them to adapt to a European-style society. A few have successfully managed to make this transition, but Australia's 386,000 Aborigines remain the most disadvantaged group in the nation. They have the highest rate of unemployment, the greatest threat of disease, and the lowest level of education in the country.

About half the Aboriginal population live in towns and cities, leading an urban lifestyle. However, most of them remain poor. In 1986 the government announced a program to advance the reconciliation process between white and Aboriginal Australians. An Aboriginal Reconciliation Council was formed, and an annual Sorry Day was set aside to acknowledge past laws and practices that brought suffering to Aboriginal people. Nevertheless, Prime Minister John Howard has refused to offer an official apology for past wrongs.

The "Aborigine question" has polarized Australian society. Those who believe that the problems faced by the Aboriginal community were caused by unfair treatment by Europeans in the past include many members of

After years of being forced to "assimilate," Aborigines are now encouraged to preserve and reinforce their unique cultural identity.

recent governments. Of the many public programs and incentives instituted to help Aborigines, one in particular—giving land held sacred by the Aboriginal community back to the Aborigines—has been enormously controversial. Opponents of the so-called "land rights" legislation claim that Australia belongs to all Australians, not just to one particular section of the community. They also point to instances of mismanagement of land already given to Aboriginal groups, including the subsequent selling of sacred land to mining companies.

Through the "land rights" program, the government aims to restore land ownership to Aborigines.

A NEED FOR KNOWLEDGE AND IDENTITY

University lecturer and author James Miller believes the current condition of the Aborigines would be greatly improved if they could raise their educational level and gain a sense of identity within their community. An Aborigine himself, Miller prefers to be known as a Koori, the Aboriginal word for Aborigines from southeastern Australia.

Miller explains that he uses the term Koori because "it's my ancestral form of identification. Also, 19th-century thinking portrayed my people as simple, barbaric and savage, using the term 'aboriginal,' and we were not those things. I really can't identify with it because it doesn't give my people a separate identity."

LIFESTYLE

"RELAXED AND FRIENDLY" is the Australian image made famous throughout the world by actor Paul Hogan, and to a large extent, this description holds true. Despite the pressures of modern society, Australians retain the old-fashioned values of hospitality, honesty, and modesty.

Australians have been described as belonging to "the 51st state of the United States" because of their close identification with American culture. This stemmed from the arrival of thousands of U.S. troops in the country during World War II. In addition to American influences on Australian fashion, food, and entertainment, the Australian lifestyle has also been shaped by Europeans and, more recently, Asians.

Left: The typical "Aussie" is a warm, casual individual who enjoys nature and outdoor activities.

Opposite: Australians are a fun-loving, colorful people.

LESSONS FROM THE SWAGMAN

During the depressions of the 1890s and 1930s, thousands of Australians, out of work and out of money, threw a few belongings in a bag, or swag, bid farewell to their families, and headed for the Outback in search of work. From these men grew the tradition of the swagman (*below*). The swagman embodies many ideals Australians greatly admire, ideals that influence Australian lives and attitudes. Here are a few of them:

- "Mateship" refers to the bonds between close friends, or mates. These bonds are extraordinarily strong among Australians. Mates are expected to look after each other in times of need. Failure to do so—letting down a mate—is considered shameful.

- "A fair go" refers to the belief that all individuals, regardless of birth or background, should be given an equal chance to succeed in whatever they choose to do.

- The imagination of the Australian public is captured by stories of "battlers," or underdogs, who fight against overwhelming odds. But, although Australians are ever willing to help those in need, they also like to see individuals who flaunt their success to be "brought down a peg or two." This is known as the Tall Poppy Syndrome.

- The "larrikin," or the rogue with a heart of gold, has a special place in Australian hearts. Famous larrikin range from actor and comedian Paul Hogan, to Bob Hawke, prime minister of Australia in the 1980s and 1990s, and Ginger Meggs, a popular cartoon character.

THE FAMILY

Like people in other Western societies, Australians live in nuclear families made up of parents, brothers, and sisters. Because of the vastness of the continent and the willingness of the population to travel in search of work or a better lifestyle, contact between members of the extended family—grandparents, uncles, aunts, and cousins—can be infrequent. Family members do, however, get together for Christmas and Easter, often traveling thousands of miles across the country to share in the celebrations and catch up on family gossip.

From an early age, children are taught to be independent and self-sufficient. Although the law recognizes youths over the age of 18 as adults by giving them the right to vote, the 21st birthday is traditionally celebrated as the day of attaining adulthood. During the course of the celebrations (which can often be quite elaborate), the birthday boy or girl is sometimes presented with the symbolic "key to the door," meaning that they are now free to come and go from the family home as they choose, thus representing the beginning of an independent adult life. Festivities are usually accompanied by much drinking, embarrassing speeches, and elaborate pranks.

Outback recreation stresses family activity. Despite the emphasis on independence and self-reliance, the family unit is still a strong pillar of society in Australia.

EDUCATION

All children between 6 and 15 years (16 in Tasmania) of age must attend school. After the first six or seven years of primary school, pupils progress to high school, where they spend a minimum of four years. Those intending to go to college or further advance their education spend an extra two years in high school in preparation for a public examination.

The school day starts between 8:30 and 9:30 A.M. and ends at 3:30 P.M., with breaks of half an hour for morning tea and an hour for lunch. Extracurricular activities like sports and music or drama may keep children at school in the afternoons or on weekends. Education is free, unless parents decide to send their children to private schools. Annual fees at private schools range from under US$390 for institutions run by the Catholic Church to over US$5,000 at the nation's top schools.

Students electing to further their education have a choice of going to a university or enrolling in Technical and Further Education (TAFE) at a technical college. The basic undergraduate course at most institutions is a bachelor degree of three or four year's duration. Fields of study with the largest number of students in 2000 were business administration and economics (24 percent), arts, humanities, social science (22 percent), and science (15 percent). Bachelor degrees in other fields, such as medicine, engineering, or law, may take up to 6 years to obtain. Government and industry provide scholarships to help students of outstanding merit.

Australian education may be described as progressive. Instead of merely teaching the "three R's" (reading, 'riting, and 'rithmetic), pupils are encouraged to think, to question, and to argue the merits of existing beliefs. Emphasis is placed on the teaching of skills that will assist students in the adult world and encourage them to make a mature contribution to society. In recent years, there has been an increasing emphasis on information technology (IT) in schools. Children are learning computer skills at a very young age.

Every year, the federal government increases its education budget by 10 percent, to provide students with the latest educational aids and technical equipment.

THE SCHOOL OF THE AIR

Children in Australia's isolated Outback who are unable to attend a regular school can instead enroll in the School of the Air. A service run by state governments, the School of the Air broadcasts lessons over the airwaves. Students participate in discussions with teachers and classmates using a two-way radio (*below*). Tests and projects are supervised by parents and mailed to the school. Electronic mail is also used to speed up communication between teachers and students. To help children with their studies, Outback parents may also employ home tutors.

Because of the great distances that often exist between teachers and students, many students of the School of the Air rarely meet their teachers or classmates in person. Camps held three of more times a year provide School of the Air students with opportunities for social interaction and exposure to cultural programs and other school activities.

WORK

It used to be the case in most Australian families that the husband worked and the wife stayed at home to look after the house and children. Changing attitudes and the rising cost of living have, however, encouraged women to return to work. Today, women make up 51 percent of Australia's workforce, and this proportion is increasing. Two-thirds of all the Australian workforce is employed in the service industry, which includes retailing, health, entertainment, education, and finance. It also includes Australia's largest employer, the Public Service, which employs one in four Australians.

In the past, long and hard battles were fought for the conditions enjoyed by workers today. Among the innovations now offered by most employers are flextime in which workers can choose the hours they work, a minimum wage in proportion to the work involved, and retirement programs to support workers when they stop working. In addition, employers must observe strict anti-discrimination laws that prevent job applicants from being rejected on the basis of race, sex, age, or physical disability. Workers' rights are further protected by unions, which are strong and well-organized. There are 275 trade unions, and one out of every two workers belongs to a union. More than 150 unions are affiliated with the Australian Council of Trade Unions, representing about 2.4 million workers.

The average Australian employee works seven to eight hours a day, Monday to Friday, and has four weeks' paid vacation a year. In recent years, more women have joined the labor force.

Most Australians stop work at about 5 P.M. Thanks to the mild climate, Australians can take part in outdoor recreational activities after work.

AN ORDINARY DAY

Most Australians lead an urban lifestyle. From Monday to Friday the urban Aussie wakes up at around 7 A.M. After a breakfast of juice, cereal, toast, or eggs and bacon, family members go their various ways to start work or attend school.

The children attend school from about 9 A.M. to 3:30 P.M. and adults work from 9 A.M. to 5 P.M. The family gathers together for dinner at about 6:30 P.M. After dinner, the children do their homework and their parents might read or watch television. Most suburban families are in bed by 10 P.M. during the week.

On the weekend, the Australian family may take part in some form of recreation, which can include a simple barbecue in the backyard with close friends or a drive to the countryside with a picnic or barbecue lunch. Being sports lovers, the Australian family may either pursue a favorite sport or watch it on television.

Elderly people live in their own homes, and the family visits the grandparents on weekends.

THE GREAT AUSTRALIAN DREAM

The most common dwellings in Australia are free-standing one-floor houses (*below*) built of brick or wood with a tiled roof, usually situated on 10,890 square feet (1,000 square m) of land. Most houses have at least three bedrooms, a living room, a kitchen and dining area, and a family, or "rumpus," room. Homes in warmer areas have open verandas that may run the length of the house. Families often sleep on the veranda on hot nights to take advantage of cool breezes. Many houses in the tropics are built on stilts. In addition to allowing better circulation of air, this feature also protects the house from floods.

The desire to own a house on a plot of land is known as the "Great Australian Dream." Although this goal does not seem particularly ambitious, it is becoming increasingly harder to realize as Australia's urban real estate becomes more and more expensive. Buyers with their hearts set on an inner-city home often have to settle for small, unrenovated houses with little or no garden. The other alternative is to move farther away from the city center, to the more affordable outskirts of the suburban sprawl. Nevertheless, three in four Australian families own their homes.

RELIGION

THE VARIOUS RELIGIOUS GROUPS in Australia are not confined to particular geographical regions. Because Australia is a secular state with no official religion, followers of all religions are free to practice their faith under the full protection of the law. Historically, it has seldom been necessary to go to court to settle religious disputes, which tend to be few due to the easygoing nature of the Australian people.

Since the Australian population is diverse, a wide variety of religions and places of worship are found throughout the country. Immigrants are encouraged to keep their own cultures, and different religious practices are viewed with tolerance, by both the government and the population.

Christianity is the major religion, but Judaism, Islam, and Buddhism also have many followers. In addition, religious sects—both Christian and non-Christian—also enjoy a following.

Although almost half the population described itself as Christian in the latest census, only one out of four attends church regularly. The Church, nevertheless, plays an important role in society, carrying out charity work and social programs.

Above: **A Buddhist temple in Sydney.**

Opposite: **A Baha'i temple in Sydney.**

St. Mary's Cathedral in Sydney. Three-quarters of the Australian population profess Christianity. One third of all Australian Christians are Anglicans and another third are Roman Catholics.

THE CHRISTIAN CHURCHES

Also known as the Church of England, the Anglican Church was the first organized church to be established in Australia. It has played a dominant role in shaping the nation's legal, social, and political institutions. Anglicans believe that religion cannot be separated from everyday life, and church leaders have a reputation for speaking out on social issues.

Australia's other major Christian religion, Roman Catholicism, was first introduced by Irish migrants in the early 19th century. More recent immigrants from Italy and Asia have strengthened the Church's numbers. Current figures indicate that one in three Australians is a Roman Catholic. Although this represents more than 6 million followers, the Roman Catholic Church has no Australian cardinal. Local policies of the Church are instead decided by a council of bishops.

Roman Catholics and Anglicans make up about two-thirds of all Christians in Australia. The remainder are mainly Presbyterians, Methodists, Lutherans, Baptists, and followers of the Eastern Orthodox Church. The Presbyterian Church is noted for its charity and missionary work—it runs the Royal Flying Doctor Service, which brings rapid medical attention to isolated families in the Outback. The Uniting Church was formed in 1977 by Methodists, Presbyterians, and the Congregational Union of Australia.

One unique Outback institution is the Royal Flying Doctor service. Started by the Presbyterian Church, it brings medical assistance to people of all religious faiths living in the remote areas of the Outback.

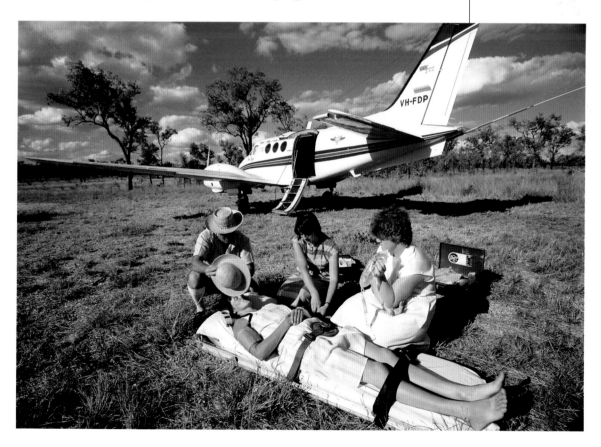

Sydney's Buddhist are mainly Asian.

JUDAISM

Judaism has a long history in Australia. Jews were among the settlers who arrived in 1788 on the First Fleet from England. The community rapidly grew after World War II due to the influx of immigrants from the former Soviet Union and other parts of Europe. Many of these immigrants were victims of religious or political persecution in their home countries. The Jewish community in Australia consists of an estimated 120,000 people. Although most Australian Jews live in Sydney and Melbourne, synagogues can be found in over a dozen different cities across the nation.

BUDDHISM

Buddhism was introduced to Australia by Asian immigrants in the latter half of the 19th century. These immigrants included Chinese laborers who came to work in the gold mines, Japanese pearl fishermen, and Sri Lankans who settled in the northern part of Australia. The first Buddhist monastery, however, was only established one hundred years later—in 1971, in the Blue Mountains region west of Sydney.

HINDUISM

Australia's Hindus are mostly immigrants from the Indian sub-continent, Southeast Asia, East Africa, and Fiji who arrived in the country in the 1970s, after Australia abolished its White Only immigration policy. The criteria for granting immigration permits at this time became very strict. Therefore, most of these immigrants were well-educated professionals. Although the Hindu community in Australia has a short history, the community has built several Hindu temples across the country. The first Hindu temple ever built in Australia, dedicated to the Hindu god Murugan, is located in Sydney.

THE SIKHS OF WOOLGOOLGA

Visitors to the coastal town of Woolgoolga will find it difficult to miss the domed white building overlooking the town. On closer inspection, they will see a notice instructing visitors to remove their shoes and cover their heads with a handkerchief before entering. This temple, known as the Guru Nanak Sikh Gurdwara, was built by the city's community of Sikhs, which make up about a third of the town's population. Sikhs first settled in Woolgoolga in the early 1900s to grow banana trees, which can be seen rising from the surrounding hills.

Guru Nanak founded Sikhism in India in the 16th century. Sikhism is a fusion of the tenets of Hinduism and Islam. Sikhs have adopted five objects as a mark of their religion: long hair, short trousers, a comb, an iron bangle, and a dagger.

The belief in one god is a basic tenet of Sikh scripture. Devout Sikhs express their worship in three ways: daily recitation of set passages of scripture, daily family worship, and regular worship at the temple.

Although they accept
Australia's secular laws,
Muslims retain their
religious customs such
as the traditional head
scarf for women.

ISLAM

Islam is one of the fastest-growing religions in Australia. It was introduced by Afghan cameliers who came to Australia in the late 1800s. The religion is founded on the Five Pillars of Islam: the worship of Allah and the belief that Mohammed was the last prophet, daily prayers, fasting during the month of Ramadan, charity, and a pilgrimage to Mecca. Australian Islam is of a liberal brand, although devotees abide by the rules of their faith. Muslim law is not officially recognized by the government.

ABORIGINAL RELIGION

Aboriginal religion centers on a spirit world known as the Dreamtime or the Dreaming. They believe that this world existed long before the coming of human beings, and that it continues to exist parallel to ordinary life. The creation of the world by spirits and creatures from the Dreamtime is told in stories passed down from generation to generation. It is also described in Aboriginal art and dance.

The Dreaming has different meanings for different Aboriginal people. It is a complex network of knowledge, faith, and practices that derive from stories of creation, and which dominates all spiritual and physical aspects of Aboriginal life. The Dreaming sets out the structures of society, the rules for social behavior, and the ceremonies performed in order to maintain the life of the land.

Aboriginal belief can be described as a sophisticated form of animism. Groups have adopted local plants, animals, and features of the landscape as sacred totems, the most important being Uluru. Uluru is believed to be the spiritual center of Australia and the source of numerous spiritual forces permeating the country.

Ayers Rock, now officially known by its Aboriginal name Uluru, is the largest free-standing monolith on earth. It is about 1.5 miles (2.4 km) long and 1,000 feet (305 m) high. The Aborigines have a religious and spiritual attachment to it.

LANGUAGE

AUSTRALIAN ENGLISH IS RICH in colorful slang and words borrowed from Aboriginal languages. While the basic structure of Australian English is the same as that of the English in other English-speaking countries, Australian English contains subtleties that sometimes baffle non-Australians.

In its written form, Australian English follows mostly British style. The Macquarie Dictionary is the authoritative guide on standard Australian spelling and words. In recent years, colloquial speech has been heavily influenced by American popular culture. Moreover, the names of many of Australia's unique flora and fauna, its geographical features, and its towns are Aboriginal words. Early Australian pioneers were obviously hard pressed to find names for their discoveries. Ernest Giles named a mountain range Ophthalmia Range, after a disease that was plaguing him at the time!

Left: **Australian English is predominantly British. Its written form, in particular, follows British style and usage.**

Opposite: **English is the language of instruction in all Australian public schools.**

Conversations are very informal, reflecting the Australian lifestyle.

CONVERSATION

The Australian accent, which is said to come from a mix of the London cockney and the Irish accent, characteristically pronounces pure vowel sounds as diphthongs (the union of two vowel sounds). The vowel sound is also sometimes changed entirely from the expected British or American pronunciation, so "day" becomes "dye" and "die" becomes "doi." The Australian accent can be heard to a greater or lesser extent throughout the country, and it gives Australian conversation a flavor of its own.

Other English speakers have in the past not taken well to the Australian accent. Local filmmakers have had to dub or subtitle their work in response to complaints from foreign audiences. In 1911 one English author went so far as to say that "the common speech of the Commonwealth of Australia represents the most brutal maltreatment which has ever been inflicted on the mother tongue of the great English-speaking nations." Harsh words indeed!

THE AUSTRALIAN UNDERSTATEMENT

Making little of major happenings is a distinguishing feature of Australian conversation. Australians do not like to dramatize events, unless they are telling one of their "tall" stories. In this case, everything is blown out of proportion. However, understatement is the more usual feature.

Districts beset by torrential rains are "having a spot of bad weather." People in serious trouble are described as "having a bit of bother," and those who have achieved outstanding success have "done all right."

"Some trouble with a steer"—the caption of this drawing is a typical example of Australian understatement.

A CRASH COURSE IN AUSTRALIAN ENGLISH

Increasingly, both spoken and written English in Australia follow American norms. Nevertheless, several uniquely Australian words and expressions are still regularly used in everyday conversations. Here are some popular ones:

"She'll be right" means "It is under control, no need to worry." If something does not go well, you can refer to it as *"a dingo's breakfast."*

"G'day mate" means "Hello friend." The word *"mate"* may be added at the end of a phrase or sentence, for example, "She'll be right, mate."

Australians call Australia *Down Under* or *Oz.* An Australian is an *Aussie.* Within Australia, citizens from Queensland are known as *banana benders,* Victorians as *Mexicans,* Western Australians as *sandgropers,* and Tasmanians as *Taswegians.* Those who live in the country's extreme north come from the *top end. True blue* or *dinki di* describes someone or something that possesses genuinely Australian qualities.

Footy means football, which in Australia refers to games played under the Rugby League or Australian Rules codes of play. Australian Rules football is also known as *Aussie Rules.*

AUSTRALIAN SLANG

Much of Australia's colorful slang dates back to the country's early days. "Bludger," a criticism leveled at those who are lazy, owes its origins to the early colony's ruthless muggers, who struck their victims with heavy sticks (bludgeons) before making away with their possessions.

Local farmers are known as "cockies," short for "cockatoo growers," since after spending a hard day sowing a field, a farmer would often wake up the next morning to find a flock of cockatoos, or Australian parrots, busily eating all his seeds. The farmer would "get his own back" by indulging in a meal of "bush mutton," or roast cockatoo! The galah, a species of cockatoo, has a reputation for being incredibly stupid. Thousands of galahs are killed each year because of their stubborn habit of pecking at live power lines. Silly people are good-naturedly referred to as "galahs."

Nicknames are an affectionate tradition in Australia. Usually, friends' names are shortened by adding an "o" to the end of the first syllable. "David" becomes "Davo" and "John" becomes "Johnno." The "o" ending is also used for other things such as coffee breaks, known as "smokos."

Australian speech is flavored with slang and many words derived from the language of the Aborigines.

Aboriginal culture once depended solely on oral tradition.

ABORIGINAL LANGUAGE

The Aboriginal groups in Australia originally spoke between them about 250 languages consisting of as many as 700 dialects. These languages were separate languages, as distinct from one another as English is from Chinese. None of the Aboriginal languages had a written script.

Clashes with the first British settlers over land ownership, as well as the diseases brought by the new settlers, wiped out a number of Aboriginal groups and their languages. It is estimated that at least 50 were irretrievably lost in this way. In the case of 100 other languages, the number of present-day speakers is so small that these languages will probably die with them. Only about 50 languages are regarded as "strong." Even then, only 20 of them are spoken by "large" groups of about 500 people.

Aboriginal languages are similar in sound and have a fairly common grammatical structure, but there are very few similarities in vocabulary. Still, there are some common words found in many of these languages, such as *jina* ("jee-nah") for foot and *mayi* ("mah-yee") meaning vegetable.

BLOKES, BLOWIES, AND BLUES

Here are some common words and phrases used by Australians:

Avago y'mug! ("Have a go, you mug!"): A frustrated plea to people, or mugs, who are not trying hard enough. Used often at sporting events.

Back of Bourke: Australia's inland, or Outback.

Bloke: A person, used in the same way as "guy" in the United States.

Blowie: A blowfly. Mosquitoes are referred to as mozzies.

Blue: An argument.

Bonza or *beaut*: Good.

Chook: A chicken, as in "running round like a chook with its head cut off," a phrase used to describe people in a state of panic.

Dobber: An informant.

Drongo or *nong*: Idiot.

Dunny: Toilet.

Fair crack of the whip: A plea for leniency.

Kangaroos in his top paddock: Not of sound mind.

Nipper: A young child, also known as an ankle biter.

Oz: Australia. Australians call themselves Aussies.

Pom or *Pommie*: An Englishman.

Stone the crows: An expression of surprise.

Tinnie: A beer can. *Grog* (alcohol), or *plonk* (wine), is drunk at pubs (bars).

Yobbos: Hooligans, also known as *hoons* and ratbags.

"I bin luk kwesjin mat" means "He was amazed" in Aboriginal Kriol.

Early European settlers recorded some words from the Dharuk, an Aboriginal group living in southeastern Australia. They included a number of words that have since been adopted into Australian English, such as "dingo," now used as the name for a species of wild dog.

For a long time, Aboriginal children attended schools taught in English. In the early 1970s, bilingual education was introduced in some Aboriginal communities. Language centers have also been set up to keep alive the Aboriginal languages. Aborigines have also incorporated some English words into their language. Aboriginal Kriol is a language spoken throughout Australia that combines English and the indigenous Aboriginal languages.

NEWSPAPERS

Australians are avid newspaper readers. It is estimated that Australians buy about 4.5 million newspapers each day and about 3 million on Sunday. The Australian press is free to express its opinions with little censorship from the government. Most newspapers have achieved a high standard of reporting, including the *Sydney Morning Herald* and Melbourne's *The Age*. Both newspapers were founded in the mid-19th century. *The Australian*, launched in 1964, is Australia's only national newspaper.

Newspapers with a large circulation, such as *The Daily Telegraph* from New South Wales, *The Age* from Victoria, and *The Courier Mail* from Queensland, are distributed throughout Australia. Each state capital has at least one morning and one afternoon newspaper.

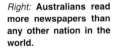

Right: **Australians read more newspapers than any other nation in the world.**

Opposite: **Radio Australia broadcasts in a number of languages to cater to the ethnic minorities.**

The *Australian Financial Review* also has a national readership. Australia has several foreign language newspapers, with the largest circulation in Sydney and Melbourne. Greek and Italian migrants have the largest number of newspapers published in their native languages.

There are also several periodicals popular with all Australians. *The Bulletin*, founded in 1880, reflects national thought and beliefs, while the *Australian Women's Weekly*, a monthly magazine founded in 1933, has a wide readership among Australian women. There are another 150 publications in almost 40 languages.

RADIO AND TELEVISION

Broadcasting and television are shared between the government-sponsored Australian Broadcasting Corporation (ABC) and a number of commercial stations. In the mid-1970s, a special service was introduced to provide programs in foreign languages for the benefit of Australia's ethnic communities. It is operated by the Special Broadcasting Service (SBS) and funded by the federal government.

ARTS

THE EARLIEST EXAMPLES of visual art in Australia date back tens of thousands of years. Created by Aboriginal artists, these sculptures and cave paintings illustrate a mythical age when spirits and fantastic beasts roamed the land. This period, called the Dreamtime, is celebrated in Aboriginal ceremonies called corroborees, in which dancers paint Dreamtime symbols on their bodies and musicians beat clap-sticks or play the *didgeridoo* ("dij-uh-ree-DOO"), a long hollow pipe made from a tree log.

Opposite: **The walls of Byron Bay's community center are decorated with original art depicting scenes of life in the town.**

Below: **Aborigine dancers perform the corroboree to the sound of the *didgeridoo*.**

The government gives full support to local artists. Artbank was created in 1980 to foster a greater appreciation of Australian art.

DESCRIBING THE LANDSCAPE

Australia's numerous art galleries are favorite attractions for both local and overseas visitors. They exhibit a diverse collection of both local and international art, including a number of works that have won the nation's most prestigious award—the Archibald Prize.

Painting the unique Australian landscape presented a major challenge to early European artists, who soon discarded the styles and rules they had learned in their homelands.

In the 1880s a new breed of landscape artists rose to the challenge. Rejecting the guidelines that were established by painters in the past, these artists, known as the Heidelberg School, used impressionistic techniques and a fresh vision to capture the essence of the country and its people in paintings of simple, everyday scenes.

The lessons learned by these Australian Impressionists influenced later artists such as Norman Lindsay, Russell Drysdale, Fred Williams, and Sir Sidney Nolan.

The *Ned Kelly* series, painted by Sir Sidney Nolan, has become as famous as Tom Roberts' *Shearing the Rams*. Nolan's works, along with those of a growing

Aboriginal art makes use of bright, warm colors and unusual shapes to convey the artist's relationship with the and and its spirits.

number of modern Australian artists, are becoming increasingly admired overseas. Pro Hart, a former miner, began painting in the 1950s. His paintings of the Australian bush have won international acclaim.

The Australian National Gallery in Canberra is world renowned for its collection of Australian art, particularly Aboriginal art.

A DREAMTIME STORY: *WHY THE STARS TWINKLE*

One night, a long time ago, some women went out to dig for yams. They dug and dug with their digging sticks. Some were lucky and found lots of yams. Others did not find any. After returning to camp, those who had yams cooked them over a fire.

The women who did not find any yams felt ashamed. They decided to live in the sky so that people all around the world could see them. But as they were rising up to the sky, the women who were eating their yams rushed to join them and went up too.

All the women turned into stars. On a clear night you can see them. The stars of those who did not find any yams are still and dim. But the lucky ones, the ones who found yams, twinkle as they eat their yams.

—from the Maung group of the Northern Territory

The Sydney Opera House is the city's most famous landmark.

A SCULPTURE THAT SINGS

The largest sculpture in Australia is 597 feet (182 m) wide and 221 feet (67 m) high. Its construction required 150 tons of concrete, 66,420 square feet (6,170 square m) of glass, 84 miles (135 km) of high-tension steel cable, and 1,056,000 tiles. It took nearly 20 years to build and cost $41 million. Within the 10 huge concrete shells that soar from its base are more than 900 rooms, including a concert hall that seats nearly 3,000 people, an opera theater, a library, and two restaurants.

The sculpture is in fact a building—the Sydney Opera House, one of the wonders of modern architecture. It was conceived in 1955, when the New South Wales state government issued a challenge to the world's best architects to design an opera house fit for its capital city, Sydney.

Jorn Utzon, a Danish architect, won the competition. His vision of huge concrete shells soaring above the harbor like the white sails of a giant

The light opera *The Gondoliers* by Gilbert and Sullivan was successfully staged at the Sydney Opera House in June 2000.

sailing ship captured the imagination of both the judges and the public. Building Utzon's dream was much more difficult, since engineers were afraid that the hall's shells would collapse under strong winds.

On October 20, 1973, 16 years after building began, the Sydney Opera House was opened by Queen Elizabeth II. Since then it has hosted hundreds of concerts, operas, plays, exhibitions, and conferences each year. Demand for the building's halls is so great that bookings must be made up to a decade in advance. Visitors to the Opera House all agree that it possesses a unique and timeless beauty. It is, in the words of its designer, "a sculpture…a living thing."

LITERATURE

Patrick White wrote many novels, short stories, plays, and poems. Although his novels are set in Australia, he writes with a wider vision, embracing universal themes.

The Outback and the exploits of its inhabitants have always been a favorite subject of Australian writers and poets. Henry Lawson wrote a number of well-loved bush stories, including *The Loaded Dog*, a tongue-in-cheek tale of a faithful retriever that—much to its owner's horror—tries to return to him a stick of dynamite with the fuse still burning!

Contemporary playwrights and authors have focused more on the attitudes and beliefs of Australians. In *The Tree of Man* (1955), Nobel Prize-winning novelist Patrick White (1912–90) ridiculed many of the qualities that Australians admire about themselves. The book sparked long and heated arguments among Australians.

Born in 1943, Victoria-native Peter Carey has won the Booker Prize, an award given annually to British Commonwealth authors, twice. His book *Oscar and Lucinda* won in 1989, and *True History of the Kelly Gang* won in 2001.

Immigrants have also contributed to Australian literature. In 1999 Hsu-Ming Teo won the Australian Vogel Literature Award for her book *Love and Vertigo*.

The country also has a long tradition of children's literature. Prominent children's writers are Ivan Southall, Patricia Wrightson, Colin Thiele, and May Gibbs.

WALTZING MATILDA: THE UNOFFICIAL ANTHEM

While most Australians do not know all the words of the national anthem, *Advance Australia Fair*, this certainly cannot be said for *Waltzing Matilda*, a poem about an Outback wanderer, a swagman, who has a run-in with the law. This simple song, known to all Australians young and old, has been suggested as a replacement to the present national anthem. Banjo Patterson is credited with writing *Waltzing Matilda*.

Once a jolly swagman
    camped by a billabong*,
Under the shade of a
    coolabah tree,
And he sang as he watched and
    waited till his billy* boiled,
"Who'll come a-waltzing
    Matilda* with me?"

Chorus
"Waltzing Matilda, waltzing
    Matilda,
"Who'll come a-waltzing
    Matilda with me?"
And he sang as he watched and
    waited till his billy boiled,
"Who'll come a-waltzing
    Matilda with me?"

Down came a jumbuck* to
    drink at the billabong,
Up jumped the swagman and
    grabbed him with glee,

And he sang as he shoved that
    jumbuck in his tuckerbag*,
"You'll come a-waltzing Matilda
    with me."

Up rode the squatter* mounted
    on his thoroughbred,
Down came the troopers, one,
    two, three,
"Where's that jolly jumbuck you've
    got in your tuckerbag?
You'll come a-waltzing Matilda
    with me."

Up jumped the swagman and
    jumped into that billabong,
"You'll never take me alive,"
    said he.
And his ghost may be heard
    as you pass by that billabong:
"Who'll come a-waltzing
    Matilda with me?"

*A billabong is a sheltered waterhole; a billy, a water can; a Matilda, a bed roll; a jumbuck, a sheep; a tuckerbag, a food bag; and a squatter, a farmer.

FILMS

Australian Mel Gibson is one of Hollywood's most popular actors.

Australia was a leading producer of movies during the era of silent films, and it holds the distinction of creating the world's first full-length feature film, *Soldiers of the Cross*. Nevertheless, after a promising start in 1896, the young local industry was soon overwhelmed by overseas productions, particularly from Hollywood. The Australian film industry virtually disappeared halfway through the 20th century because of U.S. control of the local film distribution networks.

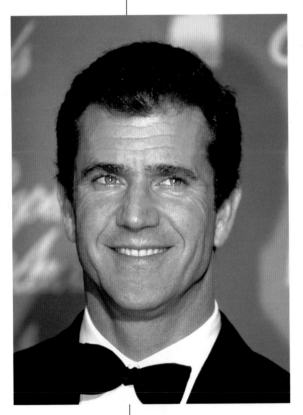

Going to the movies, however, remains a very popular pastime with Australians. Theaters come in all shapes and sizes, ranging from the city complex seating hundreds in air-conditioned comfort to the makeshift theater in the local townhall or the club auditorium of small towns.

The Australian film industry has experienced a revival in the past two decades, drawing extensively upon the work of local writers for their scripts.

Wider international recognition came with the release of *Crocodile Dundee* and its sequel, which earned its producer and star, Paul Hogan, hundreds of millions of dollars overseas. The movie grossed top dollar among local audiences, who enjoyed the stereotypical portrayal of Australia. Hogan originally worked as a rigger on the Sydney Harbor Bridge.

More recently, the Australian film industry began a resurgence that has yielded great box office hits. Leading the charge in 1979 was the *Mad Max* series starring Mel Gibson. Other Australian films that have achieved cult status in recent years include *Priscilla: Queen of the Desert, Strictly Ballroom, Babe,* and *Moulin Rouge.*

Australian actors such as Mel Gibson, Nicole Kidman, Judy Davis, Cate Blanchett, and Hugh Jackman and directors Peter Weir and Baz Luhrmann have achieved a huge international following.

Paul Hogan's big international break came when he produced and starred in *Crocodile Dundee*, a comedy adventure about the stereotypical Australian.

JUST DESSERTS

Australian audiences are well-known for their appreciation of performing artists. One artist in particular, the prima ballerina Anna Pavlova, captured the hearts of the public during her tour of Australia in the 1930s. In tribute to the brilliant dancer, a local chef created a dessert consisting of a shell of meringue filled with whipped cream and fruit. The "pavlova," as it became known, was an instant success and soon became a national dish. Australian chefs have also created desserts for two world famous Australian sopranos— Dame Nellie Melba and Dame Joan Sutherland.

LEISURE

AUSTRALIANS SPEND their free time outdoors, enjoying the country's wide open spaces and pleasant weather. On weekends and holidays, people can be seen walking in the bush, relaxing at the beach, or simply outdoors, enjoying the sunshine.

OUTDOOR LIVING

Australia's 74 million acres of protected forests are frequented by hikers, campers, and fishermen. Fly fishermen troll streams in search of elusive brown trout and rainbow trout. Those after larger catches try their hand at offshore fishing, aiming to hook shark, marlin, or tuna.

Parks and plazas are common locations for open-air rock concerts, plays, and community celebrations, and restaurants and hotels have outdoor sections for guests who wish to relax in the night air.

VACATIONS

Australians are great travelers, in their own country and overseas. Living or working overseas for a couple of years is virtually considered part of growing up. The most popular destinations for Australians going abroad are Europe and Great Britain. In addition, many also travel to the cheaper and more accesible Asian countries and islands in the Pacific.

Australians like to spend a lot of time outdoors and are spoiled by the choice of activities available. The impressive landscape and magnificent weather make taking strolls along beautiful beaches (*above and opposite*) an easily-attainable pleasure.

BEACH CULTURE

Australia boasts some of the best beaches in the world, with warm golden sand and cool turquoise water. Many of them are located in or within a reasonable distance from the capital cities. Sydney's Bondi Beach (pronounced "bohn-dye") is just 20 minutes from the city center. As the closest surfing beach to town, it attracts surf-boarders as soon as the first rays of sunlight appear. Surfer's Paradise, on Queensland's heavily developed Gold Coast, is another popular spot for local residents and tourists. The islands on the Great Barrier Reef and several others off central and northern Queensland are excellent for beach vacations and for exploring the reef, either by snorkeling or scuba-diving.

Australians have a passion for surfing. Surfer's Paradise on the Gold Coast attracts surfers from around the world.

100

CRICKET

Cricket, Australia's most popular sport, is played by millions of sportsmen each season in their backyards, open fields, and sporting ovals (flat stretches of land used for sports). Like baseball, cricket is played by two teams of 11 players, each taking turns to bat and bowl.

The fielding side's pitcher, known as the "bowler," hurls a small ball at a "wicket" located at the opposite end of a 22-yard (20-m) grassy lane called the pitch. A batsman, or striker, from the opposing team stands in front of the wicket. Another batsman, or nonstriker, stands at the other end of the pitch. The bowler's aim is to hit the wicket with the ball. The batsman's aim is to prevent this by hitting the ball. A successful hit leads to the opportunity of scoring runs, which involves the batsman and his partner (the nonstriker) running to opposite ends of the pitch.

There are 10 different ways in which a striker can be dismissed. One way is when the bowler hits and breaks the wicket. The side that scores the most runs before all players are dismissed, or "bowled out," wins.

NSON and **HEDGES** Company

Cricket is the most popular sport in Australia, both with players and spectators. Test matches and one-day internationals can attract crowds of 80,000.

CRICKET TEST MATCHES The international form of cricket is known as a Test match and is played over five days, each side getting the opportunity to bat twice. Even then, the match may end in a draw. A recent variation of the Test match, the one-day match, is a shorter but more dynamic form of the game. It is often played at night under spotlights. Both Test matches and one-day games attract huge, enthusiastic crowds, who turn out each summer to follow the fortunes of national cricketers against teams from England, India, New Zealand, Pakistan, South Africa, Sri Lanka, and the West Indies. The regular Test matches between Australia and England are of special significance, since both teams fight for The Ashes, an urn containing the ashes of a wicket symbolizing the death of England's previous dominance of cricket. Australia's women's cricket team has also made a mark in the sport by winning the World Cup in 1997.

THE LEGEND OF THE DON

Regarded at the peak of his career as the perfect Australian, Sir Donald Bradman died in 2001 at the age of 93. Known simply as the Don, the country's greatest sports hero first brought his uncanny talent with the cricket bat to national attention as a young man when he scored a century (more than 100 runs) in an inter-state match in 1927. After being included in the national team, the Don went on to score numerous centuries, double centuries, and triple centuries—scoring a total of 6,996 runs and breaking countless long-standing records along the way. Under his captainship in the 1930s and 1940s, the Australian cricket team was invincible. Bradman himself retired in 1948 with a Test-batting average of 99.9 runs, a record that has never since been matched. He was knighted in 1949.

The Don was also at the center of a bitter dispute that soured relations between Australia and England. In a desperate effort to defeat the world's greatest batsman, the captain of the English cricket team that toured Australia at the end of 1933 resorted to unusual and highly dangerous tactics. Using the tactics known as bodyline, the English bowlers were instructed to bowl their balls not at the wickets, but at the batsman's body instead. Although bodyline tactics proved to be immediately successful even against the Don, the terrible injuries suffered by the Australian batsmen caused widespread public outrage against England. Cricket, a game steeped in the venerable traditions of sportsmanship and fair play, had become a bitter war. England won the Test series, but English cricket lost the respect and admiration of the Australian people. Bodyline tactics were declared illegal the following year.

SUMMER SPORTS

TENNIS While cricket is undoubtedly the most popular spectator sport
in Australia, its claim to being the sport most Australians like to play is
being threatened by tennis. More than half a million Australians play tennis
at a competitive level, maintaining a sporting dominance that has
produced a number of international tennis superstars, including Grand
Slam winner and four-time Wimbledon champion Rod Laver, Wimbledon
champions Pat Cash, Evonne Goolagong Cawley, and John Newcombe,
and U.S. Open champions Patrick Rafter and Lleyton Hewitt. Australia's
national tennis teams have won the Davis Cup 19 times since 1950. The
Australian Open, held in the state of Victoria, is one of the four Grand Slam
events of international tennis and attracts the world's top players.

GOLF Although golf is played all year round in Australia, the major tournaments are held only during the summer. Australia is a favorite destination for avid overseas golfers who come on special golfing vacations. The country has more public golf courses than any other nation in the world. There are numerous clubs with world standard courses that are uncrowded and charge modest fees. Four-figure annual membership fees, common in the United States and Japan, are unheard of in Australia, even at the country's most exclusive golf courses. Australia's current top golfer is Greg Norman, known as the "Great White Shark." In 1999 Karrie Webb won the U.S. Golf Titleholders Championship to become one of the world's leading female golfers. Each year, Australia plays host to one of international golfing's major tournaments, the Australian Open.

Golfing in Australia is not the rich person's sport it tends to be in other countries. The clubs have well-maintained courses and charge reasonable fees.

Rugby Union attracts 100,000 players, mainly in New South Wales and Queensland. Australia is ranked highly in international Rugby Union.

SWIMMING Australians are passionate about swimming. Many Australian homes have a pool of some sort in their backyard—from large swimming pools to small inflated ones. Public swimming pools are also very popular places to meet friends during the long summer months. Freestyle swimming, also known as the "Australian crawl," was invented in Australia. Aussie swimming greats include Frank Beaurepaire, Dawn Fraser, Murray Rose, Shane Gould, and Keiren Perkins. In the 2000 Sydney Olympic Games, Ian Thorpe and Susie O'Neil, among others, won gold.

WINTER SPORTS

FOOTBALL The sports calendar in the winter months is dominated by Australia's three varieties of football: Rugby Union, Rugby League, and Australian Rules. All three variations of football can be likened to a less structured and more free-flowing version of American grid-iron football. Unlike American players, Australian players do not wear any protective clothing and must rely on their fitness, wit, and an element of luck to escape serious injury during the season.

The oldest variety, Rugby Union, used to be played on an amateur basis; it has since become a professional sport with international matches organized by the International Rugby Union. Australia is one of the world's top-ranking teams in Rugby Union, and became the world champion in 1991 by beating England and again in 1999 by beating France in the World Cup final. Rugby League, which closely resembles Union, has a strong following in the states of Queensland and New South Wales. Players sometimes switch from Rugby Union to Rugby League.

By far the most popular variety is Australian Rules, a national sport that originated in the state of Victoria. Similar to Gaelic football, it is played on an enormous oval field. Games are hard and fast, with the action shifting from one end of the field to the other in the space of seconds. Australian Rules matches can draw huge crowds of enthusiastic fans. One grand final was attended by over 110,000 spectators, or 1 percent of the nation's population at the time.

Australia's increasing concern over the safety of the football codes, as well as the growing immigrant population from southern Europe, has resulted in soccer's emergence as one of the country's largest participant sports. In addition to school and club teams, Australia has a national soccer team, the Socceroos. The high point in Australian soccer came in 1974 when they qualified for the World Cup finals in Germany. Competitive soccer is played at club level, and Australia has had a National Soccer League since 1977.

Australian Rules fans root for their favorite team—the Hawthorn Hawks.

The Australian Grand Prix brings the excitement of Formula One racing to Adelaide's residents.

NETBALL Australia's most popular women's sport, netball, was introduced to the country by the English in the early 1900s. The sport was first introduced as "women's basketball," and it is similar to that sport. In recent years, men have started joining netball teams, and the number of men netball players is increasing by the year. The Australian women's netball team has been a consistent winner of the World Netball championships.

HAVING A PUNT

At 2:40 P.M. on the first Tuesday in November each year, workers put down their tools and supervisors interrupt inspections. Across the country, eyes and ears are glued to radios and television sets to witness the running of the premier event in the national horse-racing calendar—the Melbourne Cup. Although many Australians indulge in a bet, or punt, on the outcome of the 2-mile (3.2-km) event, Cup winners are very hard to pick, and luck plays as much a hand as knowledge. This race has become an international thoroughbred classic, and no other has such a strong hold on the Australian public.

Australians are avid race-goers and meets are held all over the country at large city courses, such as Flemington and Randwick, and at numerous local courses in smaller towns. In addition to horse racing, Australians turn out to watch harness racing and greyhound races.

The Australian love of racing also extends to motor vehicles. In addition to the annual Tooheys 1,000—an endurance race dominated by locally-made cars—the country hosts U.S.-style NASCAR races and a European-based Group A production car race series. From 1985 to 1995, Adelaide, state capital of South Australia, was the scene for the final race in the international Formula One Grand Prix competition. The Grand Prix has since been moved to Melbourne, where it is held in March. Like the famous Monaco circuit, the Melbourne Grand Prix is held in the city's streets. Famous Australian Formula One world champions are Jack Brabham and Alan Jones.

Camel races are also held in Australia. The Boulia Desert Sands camel races are the most popular in the country. Held every year in July in a small town in Queensland, these camel races attract a large crowd of tourists.

Australians love betting on the outcome of any race. One of the more unusual races is the camel race.

FESTIVALS

AUSTRALIANS CELEBRATE eight national holidays a year. In addition, each state has its own holidays held at various times of the year. The two most important festivals in Australia are the two main feasts of the Christian calendar: Easter and Christmas.

CHRISTMAS

Christmas festivities begin more than a month in advance, in November, with schools and church groups staging Nativity plays celebrating the birth of Christ. Evening gatherings are held in parks to sing Christmas carols by candlelight. On Christmas Eve, churches around the country hold a midnight mass. There are also special Christmas services on Christmas Day.

Christmas Day is celebrated at home with the family and close friends. The highlight of the day for many is Christmas lunch, an extravagant affair that requires many weeks of preparation. Some still follow the British tradition of roast turkey and ham, followed by Christmas pudding, which is doused in brandy and set alight before being served. But because Christmas falls in the middle of Australia's hot summer, many families prefer to hold a barbecue in the back garden or have a meal of cold meats or seafood and salads. The afternoon is the time for a nap or a light-hearted game of cricket with the kids to recover from the elaborate lunch.

Opposite: **Australia Day celebrations culminate in a spectacular display of fireworks.**

Above: **Christmas at Bondi Beach, with an ingeniously-decorated Christmas tree.**

On Australia Day, Australians gather to watch reenactments of the first landing of English colonists in Sydney.

NATIONAL DAYS

AUSTRALIA DAY Also known as Foundation Day, Australia Day marks the anniversary of the arrival of the first British colonists (both free settlers and convicts) in Sydney Cove on January 26, 1788. The nation's birth is celebrated on this day rather than on Federation Day, the anniversary of the creation of the Federation of Australia in 1901. This is partly due to the inopportune date chosen for federation—January 1—a day traditionally reserved to recover from the excesses of New Year's Eve! Australia Day is celebrated throughout the country in open-air festivals, as this holiday falls in the middle of the summer. People gather to watch reenactments of the first landing and to take part in contests that pay tribute to the nation's culture and history. At night, fireworks light up the dusky skies high above the cities.

ANZAC DAY Every year, on April 25, Australians observe a public holiday to mark Anzac Day. This date is the anniversary of the start of Australia's most disastrous military battle—the Gallipoli campaign of World War I, in which Australian and New Zealand troops (Anzacs) suffered horrendous casualties due to the poor leadership of their British commanders.

Military services are held at dawn on Anzac Day at various war memorials. The service ends with the words "Lest we forget"—a reminder of the horrors of war and the contribution of those Australians who braved it to defend their nation. The service is followed by a parade of servicemen from the various wars Australia has fought. The last Gallipoli campaign veteran, Tasmanian Alec Campbell, died in May 2002 at the age of 103.

The War Memorial in Melbourne is an imposing monument erected in remembrance of the thousands of Australians who have died in wars.

War veterans parade down the street to commemorate Anzac Day.

THE QUEEN'S BIRTHDAY Although her actual birthday is April 21, the birthday of Queen Elizabeth II, queen of England and the head of the Commonwealth, is celebrated every year on the second Monday in June in all states except Western Australia, where it is celebrated in October. The queen delivers a birthday speech on this day.

AGRICULTURAL SHOWS

The annual agricultural show has now become a tradition of rural Australian life, although most shows take place in cities. The tradition was brought to Australia from Britain by the first settlers.

The agricultural show gives farmers the opportunity to show off their produce and catch up on the latest developments in agriculture. In

addition to the judging of livestock and crops, awards are given for homemade arts and crafts, and a number of exhibitions are staged, including demonstrations by expert shearers (known as "gun shearers") and cattle roundup competitions. These activities are accompanied by carnival rides and games. For people living in the bush, it is a wonderful opportunity to have some fun and meet new people.

Most agricultural shows are held in late summer or autumn, and most towns host one show a year. The largest show held in Australia is Sydney's Royal Easter Show. Running for one whole week in early April, the show attracts millions of visitors each year. People come to examine samples of the best farming produce in the nation and enjoy the show jumping and rodeo events. Although rodeos are relatively new in Australia, several local riders figure among the top rodeo contestants in the United States.

AG-QUIP More specialized agricultural shows include Ag-Quip, held each year in Gunnedah, a rural town in inland New South Wales. Exhibitors display an astonishing variety of farming equipment, including state-of-the-art machinery that boasts several-million-dollar price tags. The show attracts many overseas buyers looking for sophisticated and efficient methods to boost their crop production.

Several fine wine festivals are held each year to let visitors sample the products of Australia's vineyards. Australian wine is gaining worldwide recognition, and exports have increased in the past few years.

WINE FESTIVALS

Wine-producing areas host district festivals to promote their wines. These festivals, lasting up to several weeks, feature events such as outdoor picnics, wine-making demonstrations, and tours of vineyards. Free wine is also available for tasting, but enthusiastic visitors are warned to leave their cars at home or risk punishment under Australia's strict drunk-driving laws!

Barossa Valley Vintage Festival is held in South Australia's fertile Barossa Valley every April in odd-numbered years. The festival lasts one week and features over a hundred different activities, including wine tasting, delicious food, lively music, and stage performances.

ARTS FESTIVALS

Many arts festivals are held throughout the year in Australia's cities to encourage visits from overseas artists and to help develop local talent.

The best known arts festival is the Adelaide Festival of the Arts, held on even-numbered years. During the festival, which was inaugurated in 1960, local and overseas artists, performers, and musicians flock to South Australia's capital to take part in plays, concerts, streetside singing and dancing, and exhibitions.

Similar festivals are held in Melbourne (Melbourne Festival) and Sydney (Sydney Festival) each year. The Melbourne Festival, held in October, attracts leaders in the fields of theater, dance, music, opera, visual arts, and literature. Melbourne also hosts a popular comedy festival—the Melbourne Intenational Comedy Festival—every year in April. Highlights of the month-long Sydney Festival, held in January, are free open-air performances by the Sydney Symphony Orchestra and the Australian Opera Company.

The arts festivals held in Australia's major cities, treat visitors to colorful musical parades.

MUSIC FESTIVALS

Music festivals are also popular in Australia. At the beginning of each year in January, the town of Tamworth, New South Wales, hosts the Australian Country Music Festival. The festival was started in the early 1970s by a local radio deejay who referred to the town as "the country music capital of Australia." The 10-day festival attracts more than 30,000 visitors. Some of the music is authentic Australian, but many of the songs performed show the influence of American country music. Local country musicians, who enjoy a large following in Australia, compete for the coveted "golden guitar" awards given in recognition of excellence. A giant scale model of the award stands on the town's outskirts, welcoming visitors to the city.

UNUSUAL FESTIVALS

Australians will use any excuse for a party, as evidenced by some of the more unusual festivals held in the country. These include Darwin's Beer Can Regatta and the Camel Cup, a camel race held in Australia's Outback.

During the Gay and Lesbian Mardi Gras, held in Sydney in February each year, the city's homosexual community takes to the streets in outrageous costumes. They and their elaborate floats are cheered on by thousands of onlookers. In order to raise funds for this event, every October the Mardi Gras organizers hold an all-night costume party known as the Sleaze Ball.

One of the highlights of the year for Sydney's gay community is the annual Gay and Lesbian Mardi Gras. Sequins, feathers, and makeup are a must.

THE BEER-CAN REGATTA AND THE HENLEY-ON-TODD REGATTA

People take their beer drinking seriously in Darwin, in Australia's far north. In addition to being the chief city of the Northern Territory, the town is also known as the beer-drinking capital of the world since it is believed that Darwinians hold the distinction of consuming more beer per capita than residents of any other place in the world—60 gallons (230 l) a year! To keep up with the great demand, the town's breweries package their ales in the world's largest beer bottle—the half-gallon "Darwin stubbie."

Many of the drinkers in Darwin are in fact gathering the raw materials for a highly unusual race. Every August, Darwinians gather to cheer on participants in the Beer Can Regatta, a charity race. Contestants take to the water in homemade boats (*below*), ranging from simple rafts to impressive model galleons, all made from thousands of empty beer cans. The race is the highlight of a day of festivities that, of course, includes much beer drinking.

The citizens of Alice Springs, in the Northern Territory's south, also hold an annual boat race, known as the Henley-on-Todd Regatta (a name derived from the British Henley-on-Thames Regatta) in late September. Undeterred by the fact that the Todd, the "river" on which the race is held, actually contains no water, the locals sail their boats on metal tracks. Later in the day, contestants return to the dry river bed to stage mock sea battles between "pirates" and "Vikings" using bags of flour for ammunition.

FOOD

TRADITIONALLY, AUSTRALIA IS A COUNTRY of meat eaters. Australians eat more red meat per person than people in any other nation except New Zealand. This is hardly surprising considering that traditional Australian fare consists of meat for the three main meals of the day, with a breakfast of grilled lamb chops or beef steak, sausages, bacon and eggs; cold meats for lunch; and a dinner of roast or grilled lamb, beef, or pork. Meals are served with cooked vegetables and are accompanied by bread.

The influence of new cuisines and increasing health consciousness have blunted the Australian appetite for meat, although it remains the focus of most meals. Rising prices and the faster pace of modern life have also affected the traditional Sunday roast, a sumptuous lunch that takes many hours to prepare.

Left: **Lamb is the meat of choice for the majority of Australian families. The usual Sunday lunch consists of roast lamb, potatoes, and two vegetables.**

Opposite: **The Big Pineapple in Woombye, an hour's drive north of Brisbane. Almost all the pineapples produced by Australia are grown in Queensland; half of the production is exported.**

FREE RANGE BEEF

Unlike their counterparts in the United States, Japan, and other countries, Australian diners prefer beef from pasture-raised cattle (*below*) to beef from grain-fed cattle. Australians argue that cattle free to feed in pastures produce a more flavorful meat that is healthier because it contains less marbled fat.

Furthermore, many locals believe that the methods used to raise grain-fed cattle are cruel since the animals are not allowed to walk freely in the pastures and exercise. They also argue that grain-feeding methods are wasteful since the cereals used to feed the cattle could instead be made into products for human consumption.

FOOD FOR THE OUTDOORS

Camping in the Australian bush is not complete without damper and billy tea. Damper is a bread made from flour, salt, sugar, soda, and milk. The ingredients are combined and cooked in the hot ashes of an open fire until a blackened crust forms. When eaten with generous portions of treacle, a thick syrup similar to molasses, damper is known as "cocky's joy." The perfect drink to have with damper is billy tea. After water boils in a camp can, known as a billy, a few tea leaves and the odd gum tree leaf are thrown in for about a minute. The cook settles the tea leaves by tapping the billy with a stick, then grasps the handle firmly and swings the billy around in a wide circle several times to cool the tea. To avoid disaster, this last step should be left to those with experience!

Billy tea and damper— the prerequisites of life in the bush. Damper, or soda bread, was brought by early settlers who were reluctant to eat native products. Billy tea is boiled in a billy, a tin can with a lid.

The influence of immigrants from the Mediterranean has led to a widespread café culture in Australia.

FAST FOOD

Fast food, which caters to the Australian outdoor lifestyle, has grown in popularity in recent years.

Hamburgers, which were made popular by American soldiers stationed in Australia during World War II, have become a local culinary institution. Hamburgers sold at small neighborhood shops, known as corner shops, are huge, cramming a beef patty, bacon, a fried egg, cheese, onions, lettuce, tomatoes, beets, cucumber, and a slice of pineapple into a buttered bun.

Equally popular is the meat pie, a fist-sized fast food that can be eaten on the run. Originally brought from England by early settlers in the 1800s, meat pies are now viewed as Australia's national dish.

BUSH TUCKER

Unable to eke any sustenance from what they saw as the inhospitable bush, European settlers brought their crops and livestock with them. The ensuing clearing of the landscape to create pastureland resulted in environmental havoc. Today, in seeking more environmentally friendly solutions to the problem of sustaining a nation, interest is growing in the food or "bush tucker" that is provided naturally by the Australian landscape, a resource that has been exploited by the Aborigines for thousands of years. Bush tucker includes dubious delicacies such as the Witchetty grub, a fat, white slug-like creature that inhabits the bush of the same name and is traditionally eaten raw. In recent years, Witchetty grubs have been exported as "wood lobsters," with the recommendation to serve them lightly sauteed with a few herbs and spices.

Although the kangaroo formed a staple part of the Aboriginal diet, present-day Australians are generally less enthusiastic about eating the country's animal emblem. Nevertheless, kangaroo steaks and stews and kangaroo tail soups were all a popular part of Australia's recent culinary past. Kangaroo tail soup was in fact so popular in the 1960s that it was canned for export. Crocodile steaks have met with a better reception. There is an undoubted secret satisfaction in eating crocodile, since each year one or two unfortunate swimmers fall victim to these beasts.

If a crocodile or kangaroo is not handy, meals can be had from snakes, turtles, birds, all kinds of fish and eels, ants, wild bees, wild cereals and grasses, and native roots, fruit, and figs, as well as the resin from parasitic scale insects living on Mulga trees. Plants and smaller animals are often eaten raw. Larger animals are usually roasted in hot coal (*right*).

In addition to its exotic appeal, bush tucker is nutritious and tasty. Those adventurous enough to give it can visit restaurants specializing in this cuisine.

Bush tucker plants are used as food coloring and also to make jellies, seasonings, and drinks.

FAVORITE DISHES

Some foods have become so popular with Australians that they are regarded as culinary institutions, much like the hamburger.

PUMPKIN SCONES A long domestic tradition in northern Australia, pumpkin scones enjoyed a recent revival under the hands of Flo' Bjelke-Petersen, wife of former Federal Senator Joh Bjelke-Petersen. She baked vast quantities of the little snacks to sustain her husband, then premier of Queensland, through the rigors of government. The scones obviously worked, since Joh Bjelke-Petersen enjoyed an unparalleled career in Australian politics, becoming by far the longest-serving state premier in the nation's history. He was also the most flamboyant and controversial premier in modern Australian politics.

An attack of nationalism has led some Aussie restaurants to serve dishes with names like "rack of lamb Bendigo," "Hobart shoulder," and "Beaudesert lamb"—all of which are equivalent to roast lamb.

PUMPKIN SCONES

1 tablespoon butter
3 tablespoons sugar
1 beaten egg
Pinch of salt

$^1/_4$ cup milk
$^3/_4$ cup pumpkin, cooked and mashed
2 cups self-rising flour

Cream butter with sugar until mixture is white and creamy.
Add beaten egg, milk, mashed pumpkin, sifted self-rising flour, and
    pinch of salt, and mix well.
Knead mixture into smooth dough.
Roll dough to about half an inch (2.5 cm) thick and cut small circles with
    scone-cutter.
Bake in hot oven for 15 to 20 minutes.

LAMINGTONS These delicate little sponge cakes are particularly popular at festivals and shows. Made from flour, eggs, milk, sugar, butter, and vanilla, the baked cake is sliced into 2-inch (5-cm) cubes that are then dipped in chocolate. A sprinkle of coconut gives the lamington its delightful speckled look. The lamington is also connected to Queensland politics. It is said to have been created by the wife of 19th-century Queensland governor, Baron Lamington, who served the cake bearing his name to his campaign workers.

The Jolly Jumbuck in a Tuckerbag is a more stylized variation of the favorite meat pie.

The pavlova—rich in whipped cream and ice-cream—is a wonderful dessert that should appeal to anyone with a sweet tooth.

PAVLOVA The pavlova, or "pav," is a favorite dessert created in the early 1900s in honor of Russian ballerina Anna Pavlova by Western Australian chef Bert Sachse. The pavlova consists of a crisp, smooth shell of meringue, filled with whipped cream, ice-cream, and fresh fruit.

ANZAC BISCUITS First made during World War I by Australian mothers for their boys who were fighting overseas, Anzac biscuits are crisp and long-lasting. Anzac biscuits have a pleasant gingery tang since they contain ginger, coconut, brown sugar, and golden syrup. Anzac biscuits are also known for being extremely hard, and some may even double as a tent peg hammer or a heavy-duty paper weight!

VEGEMITE A thick, black yeast extract made by the Kraft Company, Vegemite is a long-time favorite sandwich filling and an ingredient in many spicy dishes. Vegemite sandwiches are best made using thick slices of freshly-baked white bread. After generously buttering the slices, apply a small amount of Vegemite. Those unacquainted with its unique flavor should then proceed with caution, taking only modest bites and having a large drink on hand to wash it down. Vegemite is definitely an acquired taste, and its immense popularity among Australians is a frequent source of wonder to overseas visitors.

VEGETABLES AND FRUIT

Vegetables grown in Australia tend to be larger than elsewhere in the world. Carrots can be more than 12 inches (30 cm) long. Tomatoes grow as big as grapefruit. One of the most popular vegetables is pumpkin, which is used in all kinds of dishes. Other popular vegetables that grow in abundance in Australia are sweet potatoes, eggplant, cucumbers, zucchini, lettuce, cabbage, beans, and peas. Bought in supermarkets or at open-air markets, vegetables are usually fresh and crisp.

Fruit is abundant and available all year round, since many varieties can be grown in various parts of the country at different times of the year. The usual ones are apples, pears, oranges, and peaches. Strawberries are at their best and cheapest around Christmas, as are plums, cherries, bananas, pineapples, and grapes. Exotic fruits like avocados, mangoes, and papayas are also available, although they are usually more expensive.

ANZAC BISCUITS

Cookies named after the Australian and New Zealand army troops that fought alongside the British in World War I. This recipe makes a dozen cookies.

2 cups rolled oats

$^1/_3$ cup shredded coconut

$^1/_2$ cup brown sugar

1 cup flour

$^1/_2$ cup plus 1 teaspoon (125 g) melted butter

1 tablespoon golden syrup

2 tablespoons boiling water

1 teaspoon baking soda

1 tablespoon ground ginger

Combine oats, coconut, brown sugar, flour, and melted butter in a large bowl. Add golden syrup. Dissolve baking soda in boiling water and add to mix. Lastly, add ground ginger to mix. Using a tablespoon, break mix into 12–15 small balls and place on a greased cookie sheet. Place in oven and bake at 350°F (180°C) for 15–20 minutes or until golden-brown and crispy.

AUSTRALIAN MEAT PIE

This recipe makes about 10 pie servings.

1 pound (500 g) ground beef
20 small mushrooms, sliced
2 tablespoons vegetable oil
Salt and pepper to taste
1 cup beef stock (or 1 beef bouillon cube
dissolved in 1 cup boiling water)

1 1/2 tablespoons flour
Ready-made puff pastry, thawed
1 egg yolk
Tomato sauce

In a frying pan, fry beef and mushrooms in oil over medium heat until browned. Add salt and pepper to taste. Add beef stock and flour and simmer until a thick gravy forms. Remove from heat and cool. Divide pastry into two portions and roll out two rounds 3/4 inch (1.5 cm) thick. Line a greased 8-inch (20-cm) diameter pie plate. Leave some pastry for top crust. Fill pie plate with beef mixture. Cover with pastry top and trim edges. Brush pastry top with egg yolk mixed with a little water. Bake in 425°F (220°C) oven until top is brown (about 5 minutes) then at moderate heat of 350°F (180°C) for 10 minutes. Pour some tomato sauce on each slice and enjoy.

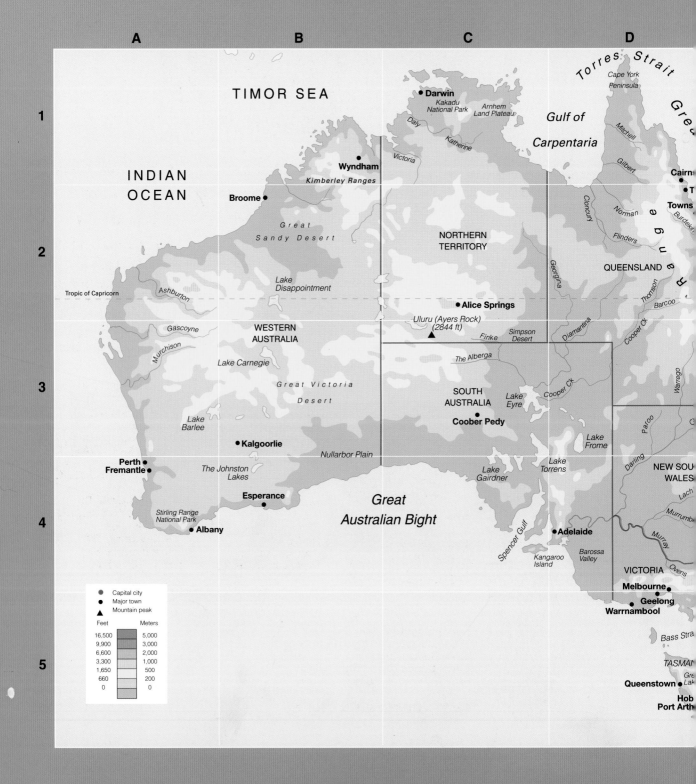

A   **B**   **C**   **D**

1

TIMOR SEA

● **Darwin**
Kakadu
National Park
Arnhem
Land Plateau

Daly
Katherine

Victoria

Gulf of
Carpentaria

Cape York
Peninsula

Torres Strait

Gre

Mitchell

INDIAN
OCEAN

● **Wyndham**
Kimberley Ranges

Gilbert

Cairns

● **T**

Cloncurry

Norman

Towns

● **Broome**

Great
Sandy Desert

Burdekin

2

NORTHERN
TERRITORY

Flinders

QUEENSLAND

Tropic of Capricorn

Ashburton

Lake
Disappointment

Georgina

Thomson

Barcoo

Gascoyne

WESTERN
AUSTRALIA

● **Alice Springs**

Uluru (Ayers Rock)
(2844 ft)
▲

Finke

Simpson
Desert

Diamantina

Cooper Ck

Warrego

Murchison

Lake Carnegie

The Alberga

3

Great Victoria
Desert

SOUTH
AUSTRALIA

Lake
Eyre

Cooper Ck

Paroo

Lake
Barlee

● **Coober Pedy**

Lake
Frome

Darling

NEW SOU
WALES

● **Kalgoorlie**

Nullarbor Plain

Lake
Torrens

Perth ●
Fremantle ●

The Johnston
Lakes

Lake
Gairdner

Murrumbe

● **Esperance**

4

Stirling Range
National Park

Great
Australian Bight

Spencer Gulf

● **Adelaide**

Murray

Lach

Ovens

● **Albany**

Kangaroo
Island

Barossa
Valley

VICTORIA

Melbourne ●

● **Geelong**

Warrnambool

Bass Stra

5

TASMAN

Gre

Lak

Queenstown ● **Lak**

Hob
Port Arth

Legend:
● Capital city
● Major town
▲ Mountain peak

Feet	Meters
16,500	5,000
9,900	3,000
6,600	2,000
3,300	1,000
1,650	500
660	200
0	0

MAP OF AUSTRALIA

ECONOMIC AUSTRALIA

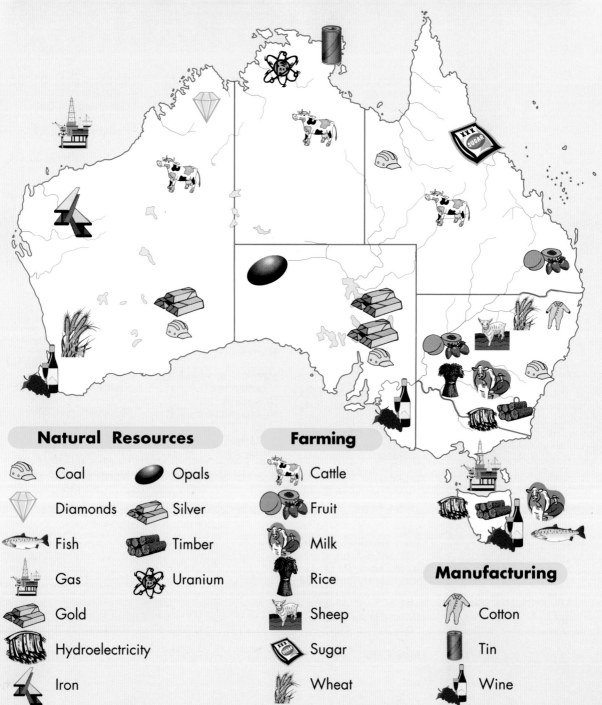

Natural Resources

- Coal
- Diamonds
- Fish
- Gas
- Gold
- Hydroelectricity
- Iron
- Opals
- Silver
- Timber
- Uranium

Farming

- Cattle
- Fruit
- Milk
- Rice
- Sheep
- Sugar
- Wheat

Manufacturing

- Cotton
- Tin
- Wine

ABOUT THE ECONOMY

OVERVIEW

Australia's capitalist economy depends heavily on the export of agricultural products, minerals, metals, and fuels. Commodities account for 57 percent of total exports, so a decrease in world commodity prices can have a big impact on the country's economy. The government is pushing for increased exports of manufactured goods, but competition in international markets continues to be severe. While Australia suffered from the worldwide low growth and high unemployment of the early 1990s and during the recent Asian economic crisis, the economy grew at a steady annual rate of 4 percent.

GDP
$445.8 billion (2000)

GDP PER CAPITA
$21,881 (2001)

GDP SECTORS (1999)
Agriculture: 3 percent
Industry: 26 percent
Services: 71 percent

CURRENCY
1 USD = 1.92 AUD (Jan 2002)
Notes: $5, $10, $20, $50, $100
Coins: 5 cents, 10 cents, 20 cents, 50 cents, $1, $2

WORKFORCE
9.5 million (1999)

UNEMPLOYMENT RATE
6.4 percent (2000)

INDUSTRIES
Chemicals, food processing, manufacturing of industrial and transportation equipment, mining, steel.

AGRICULTURAL PRODUCTS
Barley, fruit, sugarcane, wheat.

ANIMAL PRODUCTS
Cattle, poultry, sheep.

MAJOR EXPORTS
Aluminum, coal, gold, iron ore, machinery and transportation equipment, meat, wheat, wool.

MAJOR IMPORTS
Computer and office machines, crude oil and petroleum products, machinery and transportation equipment, telecommunications equipment.

MAJOR TRADING PARTNERS
ASEAN, China, EU, Hong Kong, Japan, New Zealand, South Korea, Taiwan, United States.

TRANSPORTATION
Number of airports: 411
Railways: 21,015 miles (33,819 km)
Highways: 567,338 miles (913,000 km)

CULTURAL AUSTRALIA

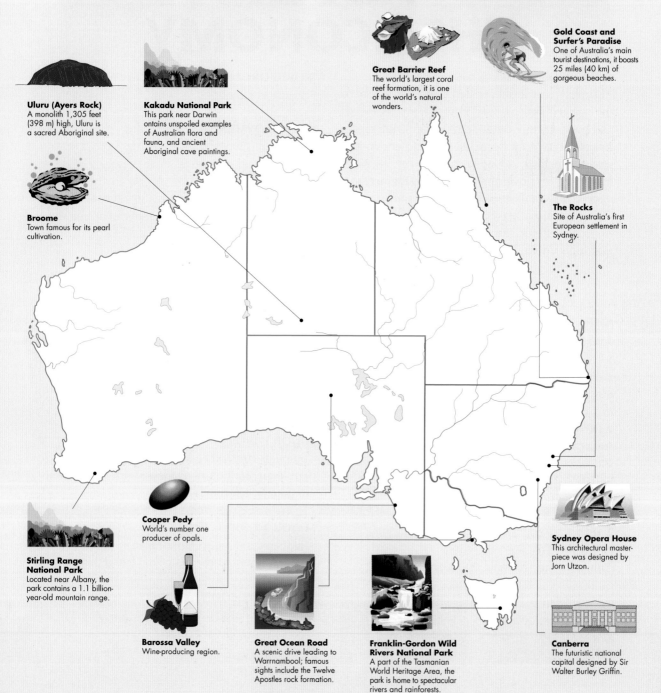

Uluru (Ayers Rock)
A monolith 1,305 feet (398 m) high, Uluru is a sacred Aboriginal site.

Kakadu National Park
This park near Darwin ontains unspoiled examples of Australian flora and fauna, and ancient Aboriginal cave paintings.

Great Barrier Reef
The world's largest coral reef formation, it is one of the world's natural wonders.

Gold Coast and Surfer's Paradise
One of Australia's main tourist destinations, it boasts 25 miles (40 km) of gorgeous beaches.

Broome
Town famous for its pearl cultivation.

The Rocks
Site of Australia's first European settlement in Sydney.

Stirling Range National Park
Located near Albany, the park contains a 1.1 billion-year-old mountain range.

Cooper Pedy
World's number one producer of opals.

Sydney Opera House
This architectural masterpiece was designed by Jorn Utzon.

Barossa Valley
Wine-producing region.

Great Ocean Road
A scenic drive leading to Warrnambool; famous sights include the Twelve Apostles rock formation.

Franklin-Gordon Wild Rivers National Park
A part of the Tasmanian World Heritage Area, the park is home to spectacular rivers and rainforests.

Canberra
The futuristic national capital designed by Sir Walter Burley Griffin.

ABOUT THE CULTURE

OFFICIAL NAME
Commonwealth of Australia

CAPITAL
Canberra

DESCRIPTION OF FLAG
Blue background with Southern Cross on right, Union Jack on top left corner, and single star on bottom left.

GOVERNMENT
Federation of states with a parliamentary government, with the British monarch as head of state.

NATIONAL ANTHEM
Advance Australia Fair

POPULATION
19.4 million (July 2001)
Population growth rate: 0.99 percent (2001)

ETHNIC GROUPS
Caucasian: 92 percent
Asian: 7 percent
Aboriginal and other: 1 percent

RELIGION
Catholic: 26 percent
Anglican: 26.1 percent
Other Christian: 24.3 percent
Others: 22.6 percent

LIFE EXPECTANCY
Male: 77 years (2001)
Female: 83 years (2001)

LITERACY RATE
99.9 percent

LEADERS IN SPORTS
Cathy Freeman, track Olympic gold medalist; Patrick Rafter, Lleyton Hewitt, tennis players; Shane Warne, Steve Waugh, cricket players; Ian Thorpe, Susie O'Neill, Grant Hackett, swimming Olympic gold medalists; Mark Viduka, soccer player.

LEADERS IN LITERATURE
Peter Carey, Bryce Courtenay, Kate Grenville, David Malouf, Druscilla Modjeska, Frank Moorehouse, Tim Winton.

NATIONAL HOLIDAYS
Jan. 1—New Year's Day
Jan. 26—Australia Day
Mar./Apr.—Good Friday, Vigil of Easter, Easter Monday
Apr. 25—Anzac Day
Early June—Queen Elizabeth's birthday
Dec. 25—Christmas Day
Dec. 26—Boxing Day

TIME LINE

IN AUSTRALIA	IN THE WORLD
40,000 B.C. First Aboriginal Australians arrive.	
	753 B.C. Rome is founded.
	116–17 B.C. The Roman Empire reaches its greatest extent under Emperor Trajan (98–17 B.C.).
	A.D. 600 Height of Mayan civilization
	1000 The Chinese perfect gunpowder and begin to use it in warfare.
1500s–1600s Portuguese and Dutch explorers visit Australia.	
	1530 Beginning of trans-Atlantic slave trade organized by the Portuguese in Africa.
	1558–1603 Reign of Elizabeth I of England
	1620 Pilgrim Fathers sail the Mayflower to America.
1770 Captain James Cook maps the eastern coast of Australia and claims it for England.	
	1776 U.S. Declaration of Independence
1788 First European settlers arrive in Botany Bay on First Fleet from England.	
	1789–99 The French Revolution

IN AUSTRALIA	IN THE WORLD
1829 Western Australia is founded as an English colony.	
1850s Discovery of gold in New South Wales and Victoria leads to "gold rush."	
	1861 The U.S. Civil War begins.
	1869 The Suez Canal is opened.
1894 Women gain right to vote in South Australia.	
1901 States unite under the Commonwealth of Australia on January 1.	
	1914 World War I begins.
1915 Heroic ANZAC campaign against Turks in Gallipoli during World War I	
1939 Australia enters World War II.	**1939** World War II begins.
	1945 The United States drops atomic bombs on Hiroshima and Nagasaki.
	1949 The North Atlantic Treaty Organization (NATO) is formed.
1956 Melbourne hosts Olympic games.	**1957** The Russians launch Sputnik.
	1966–69 The Chinese Cultural Revolution
1975 Labor government is dismissed by governor-general.	**1986** Nuclear power disaster at Chernobyl in Ukraine
	1991 Break-up of the Soviet Union
1992 The High Court's Mabo decision extends Aboriginal land and customary rights.	
2000 Sydney hosts Olympic games.	**1997** Hong Kong is returned to China.
	2001 World population surpasses 6 billion.

GLOSSARY

Aborigines
Earliest inhabitants of Australia.

artesian wells
Wells located under a layer of impermeable rock in which water rises continuously under pressure.

billabong
A sheltered waterhole.

billy
A cylindrical container with a close-fitting lid.

bush
Countryside.

colloquial speech
Speech used in informal conversation.

corroborees
Sacred Aboriginal ceremonies in which dancers paint Dreamtime symbols on their bodies.

didgeridoo ("dij-uh-ree-DOO")
An Aboriginal wind instrument consisting of a hollow pipe made from a tree log.

jumbuck
Sheep.

Koori
Word used by Aborigines to describe themselves.

matilda
Bed roll, usually carried by swagmen.

nipper
A young child.

Outback
Remote, sparsely-populated Australian country region.

over
The six throws taken by a bowler in a cricket Test match before changing ends or bowlers.

preferential voting system
The voting system used in all Australian elections in which voters must state their order of preference for all candidates, from their first to their last choice.

squatters
People who settled on land belonging to the state to raise animals.

stations
Sheep farms.

swagman
Person who roams the Outback in search of work.

tinnie
A can, usually of beer.

transportation
A system of punishment in which criminals and convicts, mainly from Britain and Ireland, were exiled to Australia from the late 18th to the early 19th century.

FURTHER INFORMATION

BOOKS

Beaglehole, J.C., et al. *The Journals of Captain Cook* (abridged). New York: Viking Penguin, 2000.

Bryson, Bill. *In a Sunburned Country.* New York: Broadway Books, 2001.

Davidson, Robyn; Rick Smolan (photographer). *From Alice to Ocean: Alone Across the Outback.* Boston: Addison-Wesley Publishing, 1994.

Duncan, Ken. *The Great Southland.* Australia: Ken Duncan Panographs, 1999.

Hughes, Robert. *The Fatal Shore: The Epic of Australia's Founding.* New York: Random House, Inc., 1988.

Iriwn, Steve, and Terri Irwin. *The Crocodile Hunter: The Incredible Life and Adventures of Steve Irwin.* New York: Dutton Books, 2001.

MacIntyre, Stuart. *A Concise History of Australia.* Australia: Cambridge University Press, 2000.

Morphy, Howard. *Art from the Land: Dialogues with the Kluge-Ruhe Collection of Australian Aboriginal Art.* Charlottesville: University Press of Virginia, 2000.

North, Peter. *Countries of the World: Australia.* Singapore: Times Editions, 1998.

O'Byrne, Denis, et al. *Lonely Planet Australia.* Australia: Lonely Planet, 2000.

Smith, Roff Martin, and Sam Abell (photographer). *Australia: Journey Through a Timeless Land.* New York: Simon & Schuster, 2000.

WEBSITES

About Australia. www.about-australia.com

Australian Bureau of Statistics. www.abs.gov.au

Official site of the Australian Tourist Commission. http://australia.com

Australia Online. www.australia-online.com

Australia's World Search Engine. www.aaa.com.au/A_Z

Department of Foreign Affairs and Trade. www.dfat.gov.au

Lonely Planet World Guide: Destination Australia.
     www.lonelyplanet.com/destinations/australasia/australia

Australian Museum Online: Indigenous Australia. www.dreamtime.net.au

VIDEOS

Amazing Australia. BFS Entertainment & Multimedia, 2000.

Amazing Wonders of the World: Island Continent–Australia. Questar, Inc., 1999.

G'Day Australia: Like Nothing Else on Earth. Paramount Studio, 1989.

National Geographic's Australia's Great Barrier Reef. National Geographic, 2000.

BIBLIOGRAPHY

Horne, Donald. *The Story of the Australian People*. Sydney, Australia: Reader's Digest, 1985.

Kelly, Andrew. *Australia*. New York: Bookwright Press, 1989.

Lawson, Henry. *The Bush Undertaker and Other Stories*. Sydney, Australia: Angus & Robertson, 1970.

Luling, Virginia. *Aborigines*. Englewood Cliffs: Silver Burdett, 1979.

Nicholson, Margaret. *The Little Aussie Fact Book*. Australia: Penguin Australia, 2000.

Stark, Al *Australia: A Lucky Land*. Minneapolis: Dillon, 1987.

Australia in Pictures. Minneapolis: Lerner Publishing Co., 1990.

The World Factbook. Washington, D.C.: Central Intelligence Agency, 2001.

INDEX